Chicago Lincoln Statue, Lincoln Square

Mrs. O'Leary's
COMET

Cosmic Causes of the Great Chicago Fire

by Mel Waskin

Academy
Chicago
Publishers

Published in 1985 by

Academy Chicago Publishers
425 N. Michigan Ave.
Chicago, Illinois 60611

Printed and bound in the USA

Pro5013778✓

Library of Congress Cataloging-in-Publication Data

Waskin, Mel.
    Mrs. O'Leary's comet.

    Bibliography: p.
    1. Fires—Illinois—Chicago.   2. Comets—1871.
3. Chicago (Ill.)—History—To 1875.
I. Title.
F548.42.W16.   1985   977.3'11041   85-18532
ISBN 0-89733-167-2
ISBN 0-89733-181-8 (pbk.)

*To my wife, Tamara, the heart of my personal comet,
and to our children, Laurie, Alan and David,
following their own luminous paths.*

Table of Contents

Introduction

In 1883 Ignatius Donnelly wrote a book called *Ragnarok: The Age of Fire and Gravel*, in which he put forward the theory that the massive deposits of clay and gravel existing in much of the world were not the result of glacial movement, as scientists of his day tended to believe, but had, instead, been created through a vast cosmic catastrophe: the collision of the earth with a comet. Thus the "Gravel" of his title. He was convinced further that this collision had produced conflagrations throughout the world: holocausts of calamitous proportions that could have eliminated the human species. This was the "Fire." He relied on physical evidence for the existence of gravel. But for evidence of the catastrophic fire he called upon the myths and legends imbedded in the memory of humankind.

He interpreted these myths not as stories of gods at play with the fate of men, but as eye-witness accounts of actual cosmic occurrences that laid waste the earth in the distant past. These were catastrophes of almost unimaginable destructiveness which passed gradually from the realm of reality to the realm of myth as generation succeeded generation. In an age of science, Donnelly had the temerity to suggest that myth had historic bases and that both pagan myth and the Bible accurately reported actual events witnessed by people in the prehistoric past.

There was little response to Donnelly's book. But one hundred years later when Velikovsky put forth similar theories, the scientific community exploded with an intellectual violence comparable in some ways to the ancient disasters Velikovsky was discussing.

The theory that planetary history may not have slowly evolved but may have occurred through sudden, vast change, is called "catastrophism." It is a theory which seems to be popular in cycles. It was for decades an accepted way of looking at natural history; and then it was rejected. Today it is once more acceptable. The scientific community is currently more or less in agreement that a collision with an asteroid about 65 million years ago caused the destruction of the dinosaur. Accepted also now is the idea that the sudden repeated disappearance and reversal of the earth's magnetic field can allow radiation to pour in on living things on the earth's surface and destroy them or change them permanently. These ideas were ridiculed when they were first proposed.

Do the continents drift? It's an acceptable idea now, but it wasn't a generation ago. Thus fashions change. Yesterday's wild theory can become today's sacred cow and tomorrow's superstition.

In 1970, in the midst of the Velikovsky furor, Donnelly's book was reprinted. I came across it on a bookstore remainder table in 1982 and was struck by the similarity between Donnelly's ideas, and those of Velikovsky, whom I admire. And I was particularly struck by a question Donnelly asks toward the end of *Ragnarok*, after he has expounded his theory that legends are an actual, if embroidered, record of a cosmic event. "Has such a cosmic event occurred within our own memories?" he asks, at the beginning of his chapter called "Biela's Comet," and he goes on to say:

> There is reason to believe that the present generation has passed through the gaseous pro-longation of a comet's tail, and that hundreds of human beings lost their lives, somewhat as they perished in the Age of Fire and Gravel, burned up and poisoned by its exhalations.
>
> And although this catastrophe was upon an infinitely smaller scale than that of the old time, still it may throw some light upon the great cataclysm. At least it is a curious story with some marvelous features.

Donnelly goes on to say that there is strong evidence that on October 8, 1871, the earth had collided with a comet or part of a comet and that the result was not only the Chicago Fire, but two other incredibly destructive fires in Wisconsin and Michigan that had, apparently through strange coincidence, begun at the same hour on the same night. That coincidence, along with eyewitness reports of unusual aspects of the three fires, caused Donnelly to think that these events might support his theories.

Apparently few people accepted his interpretation of these fires in 1883. But when I read his book I felt it deserved extensive treatment. So I began to investigate. I found the book on which he had based his theory, and it seemed to me that he had accurately extracted some unusual facts from a mass of information. Then I looked into other books containing eyewitness reports of the Chicago and Midwest fires (as they were called) and found apparently inexplicable events, conditions and circumstances that raised provocative questions.

Basically my question is: Did a dying comet collide with the earth on October 8, 1871, and fuel three vastly destructive fires? I can't say that what follows here will prove conclusively that such an event took place. But the information I have found certainly raises some interesting questions, and I invite you to believe, as I do, based on the evidence, that not a cow, but a comet caused the great Chicago Fire.

Mel Waskin
Chicago, Illinois
September, 1985

1

Biela's Comet

For thousands of years the sight of comets in the sky had struck terror into the bosoms of earthly viewers. These sudden bright streaks of light were thought to be omens of dreadful events: the deaths of kings and emperors, the destruction of cities, the failure of crops. Ancient astronomers had attempted explanations of them, but it was in 1609, when Galileo constructed the first simple telescope, that a giant step was taken toward the orderly study of celestial phenomena. In 1705, Edmund Halley, once assistant to Sir Isaac Newton whose theory of gravitational pull was itself a contribution toward understanding of astronomy, made public his belief that many comets which had been noted by observers through the years were often the *same* comet, following an orbit through space, around the Sun, and back; that four comets, seen in 1456, 1531, 1607 and 1682, were in actual fact one comet which returned every seventy-five or seventy-six years. Thus, he said, the Comet which he had seen in 1682 would return in 1758. Although he did not live to see it, his prediction was correct.

Thus tracked, charted and often named, comets, by the eighteenth century, had become interesting objects of study to amateur as well as professional astronomers.

On March 8, 1772, in Limoges, a French observer named J.L. Montaigne saw a faint comet and tracked it until March 20; the same comet was seen also by Charles Messier four times between March 26 and April 3 of that year. Both men believed it was a new comet, but neither had sophisticated enough equipment for careful study.

On November 10, 1805, the Comet was discovered again by the astronomer Jean Louis Pons, and in 1810 Friedrich Bessel, checking the orbit of Montaigne's Comet, decided that it must be the same comet Pons had seen in 1805. He predicted that it would return in 1826.

In that year, Wilhelm von Biela, a captain in the Austrian Army who as an amateur astronomer was aware of Bessel's prediction, began a watch for the Comet from his home in Josephstadt in what was then called Bohemia. On February 27, 1826, he spotted the Comet, and tracked it for twelve weeks. He calculated its orbit and decided that it was the Comet seen originally in 1772 and referred to by Bessel. Von Biela worked out its period at six years and nine months. Because of this the comet is called Biela's Comet, although it was also seen ten days later by a French astronomer named Adolphe Gambart, and the French have therefore called it Gambart's Comet. It was, strictly speaking,

Montaigne's Comet.

In any case, the astronomer Santini announced that the Comet's period in 1826 was 2455 days, but its path past Earth, Jupiter and Saturn would subject it to gravitational pulls that would probably hasten its return by more than ten days.

Biela's Comet, like most comets, resembled a hazy star — a point shrouded in a mist of glowing fog, moving slowly across the sky. It traveled, at a speed of about a mile a second, a path called an ellipse from a point in the Solar System farthest from the Sun (aphelion) to a point closest to the Sun (perihelion) and then around the Sun and back along its path again. Comets do not travel the flat plane of the skies as the planets do, and there is no definite information about their origin.

Our best guess is that the Solar System was once a globular gaseous mass in which gradually internal eddies formed that became protoplanets, leaving behind a gaseous halo as a sort of echo of the mass it once was.

This halo, an apple peeling of cosmic proportions, drifted slowly around the condensing nebula, unaffected by the aggregations and accretions that were shaping the internal eddies. The particles at the outer edges of the system, obeying the universal dictum that everything turns, moved also, remaining uninvolved in the profound changes taking place deep in the cloud of which they had once been integral parts.

At the center of the mass a star eventually began to burn with nuclear fire. Thus the Sun was born. The eddies that had formed their own flattened spirals of gas became planets, moving in precise orbits around this Sun. Now a nuclear star and a family of planets inhabited the relatively small region in one part of a galaxy where before only a gaseous nebula had been. And at its outermost limits, remnants of the dust and gases that had made up the nebula still moved slowly, in a primitive state. That is, they had not succumbed to the forces which had created the central star and planets.

However, they were undergoing changes out there, in the great circular drift. There were accumulations and compactions there, and further compactions, as small masses collided and unified with each other into larger masses. So over the billions of years during which the Sun and the planets were forming, smaller bodies were taking shape on the periphery of what was to be called the Solar System.

During the transfers and transformations of energy, elemental chemicals interacted; compounds formed of carbon, hydrogen, and oxygen. Atoms unified with each other, water formed in crystals locking other elemental compounds into balls of rock-ice, and accretions of these balls became bodies of considerable size. They grew too from the accumulation of bits of dust and gas which remained from the cosmic cloud that had existed before the birth of the Solar System. They followed their courses, just as the planets did, but the Sun's gravitational hold on them was tenuous. These bodies were subject to competing gravi-

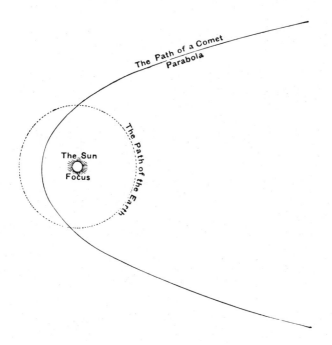

The Parabolic Path of a Comet.

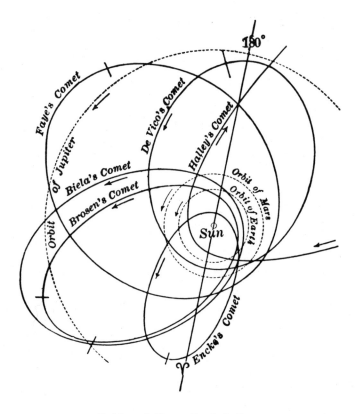

Orbits of Short-Period Comets.

tational forces, from the Sun and from the star nearest to them.

Any collision, any change in mass, would alter their speed and their path. If the speed of their movement increased, they could leave the Solar System and enter the domain of another powerful star. Anything that slowed them down would cause these bodies to fall from their haloes of drifting residue and move in a gravitational curve "down hill" toward the Sun in a new and different orbit. Then, no longer out of gravitational touch with the planets, the bodies would move through planetary space, at times crossing the planets' orbits. Because of the immensity of space, and the relative smallness of congregations of planets, there was little danger to either planet or falling body in this rearrangement of paths.

In any case, it is believed that comets are bodies that are dislodged for some reason from the halo of gases at the edges of the Solar System and which begin then a long journey around the Sun. It is not an orderly, confined journey, and often through most of it the comet is invisible from Earth. It is partly their apparent unpredictability that made comets so frightening to ancient peoples.

Their shapes too, are irregular, although certain of the parts are distinct. Each comet has a head, a central bright region called the nucleus, which can on the average be some ten or twenty miles in diameter. From Earth, the nucleus resembles a bright star. The misty aura in which the nucleus resides is called the coma. It is tenuous, being made up, apparently, of layers of dust. The full head of the comet — the starry nucleus set into the misty coma — appears to vary widely in size in various comets: from twenty thousand to one million miles in diameter. The tail of the comet emerges from the coma.

Long before the comet passes Jupiter on its way to the Sun, the tail is born. It grows little until the comet reaches the orbit of Mars, when the energy of the Sun begins to have a significant effect upon it. At its fullest, the cometary tail is seldom less than five or ten million miles long, and is frequently as long as fifty million miles. In rare cases it can reach a hundred millon miles or longer. Needless to say, these long-tailed comets are magnificent sights. As they approach the Sun they brighten gradually because they absorb solar energy.

In the coma are clusters of particles: bits of rock and metals, and icy chunks of water, ammonia, methane, acetylene and other carbon compounds. The outer layers of slush evaporate as solar energy pours into the coma. The gases and tiny particles that were frozen together into a kind of "snowball" are released and driven away from the main body of the coma by the pressure of sunlight and by solar wind, which is the stream of particles given off by the Sun. As the comet comes closer to the Sun, these gases and particles stream out behind the coma and form the immense, awesome, glowing tail, which always points away from the Sun and which,

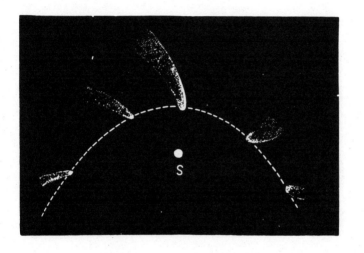

*A Comet's Tail at Different Points
in its Orbit near Perihelion.*

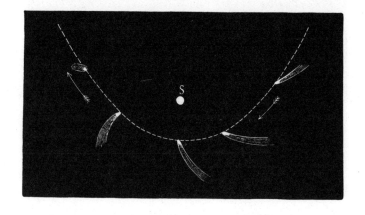

*The Tail of a Comet directed **from the Sun**.*

when stretched out for millions of miles, becomes insubstantial indeed. When the comet rounds the Sun and moves back along its path, the tail moves with it, and continues to point away from the Sun, because the comet is moving in a vacuum and the tail is responding to the force of the solar wind.

As the comet passes perihelion it loses some of its aura, which is vaporized by the Sun. Thus it has been suggested that a comet like Biela's, which rounds the Sun fairly frequently, cannot live as long as a comet like Halley's, which reaches perihelion only every seventy-five odd years, or like those comets which, instead of following ellipses — paths within the Solar System which lead the comets round the Sun at intervals within possible human lifespans — follow parabolas, or curves so great that the comet would reach perihelion once in perhaps a million years, or more.

Biela's Comet, when it was seen in 1826, was expected to return in November of 1832, and to reach perihelion on November 27 of that year. A German astronomer named Heinrich Wilhelm Olbers said that in its 1832 approach it would, on October 29, pass very close to Earth's orbit. He added that of course Earth would at that time not be in that part of the orbit but would be fifty million miles away from it. Man's basic perception of comets as harbingers of evil flared up wildly at Olbers' announcement, and there was a widespread conviction that on October 29, 1832, the Comet would collide with the Earth.

Astronomers hastened to pour oil on these troubled waters, and to explain that at the moment that Biela came near the Earth — and "near" meant within twenty thousand miles of Earth's orbit — Earth itself would have been gone from that particular spot for more than a month. The public at large accepted this reassurance and the panic abated. In 1832 the Comet did come close to Earth's orbit, and there was in fact no danger to Earth.

Nevertheless, astronomers were aware that a collision between Earth and a comet was more than a possibility; it was a probability. There were already in the nineteenth century several known comets the orbits of which would come closer to Earth's orbit than the radius of the comet's head. If both Earth and these comets — including Biela's — maintained their paths through space at their calculated speeds, there was sure to be an eventual collision. There was also, of course, the very real possibility that the gravitational forces of the universe could pull a comet out of its accustomed path at any time, and increase or decrease its speed with catastrophic effects. It was even possible that this dreadful cosmic accident had actually occurred in the dim reaches of the past.

Astronomers in 1828 did not know enough about the consistency of comets to visualize the result of such a collision with any kind of authority. They did believe, however, that the effect of the collision would depend upon the mass of particles that formed the nucleus of the comet.

If the weight of these particles was in the range of a considerable number of tons, the collision would be a real catastrophe. If, on the other hand, the particles were merely the size of pinheads, then the likely result of a collision would be a meteor shower of unusual beauty. In any case, it was added, such collisions would in all likelihood occur perhaps once in fifteen million years. It was granted that no one knew when the last one had occurred, but in terms of earthly reckoning, the danger did not appear to be imminent.

On August 23, 1832, Biela's Comet was first seen by an observer in Rome: it was quite faint. It rounded the Sun in November. Astronomers were then considerably distracted by Halley's Comet, which returned and passed perihelion on November 27, 1835. After that attention was once more fixed on Biela, which, as a frequent visitor, coming quite close to Earth, could be satisfactorily studied at length. In July 1839 the Comet was seen, but its perihelion passage was missed because it was moving too close to the Sun. Nevertheless it had proved itself a faithful follower of astronomical calculations and an interesting addition to the family of named and charted comets. No one expected that it would prove to be anything else — at least for several million years.

2

Chicago, 1833

In 1833 the town of Chicago covered a small area of land on either side of the Chicago River at the point where it became part of Lake Michigan. The River was fed from two branches — a North and a South branch — barely a mile from the Lake. The River and its branches divided the city into three natural parts: South, North and West divisions.

Little is known of Chicago's history from 1681 to 1795 during the time of its possession by France and its cession to England. When peace was declared between England and its former colonies, the English stirred up border Indian warfare, which spread throughout the Western territories, continuing until 1795 when it was put down by General Wayne. At the General's invitation, the chiefs of several of the warring tribes met with him at Greenville, Ohio, and drew up a peace treaty in which the Indians ceded to the Federal Government rights to much of their land. Among these numerous small tracts which held forts and trading posts was this one:

One piece of land, six miles square, at the

mouth of the Chikajo River, emptying into the southwest end of Lake Michigan, where a fort formerly stood.

This was Chicago, and the treaty was the first land transaction in Chicago.

The first settlers of Chicago, including Jean Baptiste Pointe du Sable, built their cabins on a tract of land on the West Side, at the junction of the North and South branches of the River: this area was called Wolf's Point. In 1804 the Federal Government erected Fort Dearborn on the South bank of the River, just east of what was to become Michigan Avenue. The area was hardly bustling: until the War of 1812 the only white residents were James Kinzie and his son John H., who traded with the Indians. When the War began, a small garrison was sent to man the Fort from which they were, in the course of events, forced to flee. The garrison was caught and massacred by Pottawatomi Indians at a point which was later to become Twelfth Street — or Roosevelt Road — and Michigan Avenue.

In 1816, however, the Fort was rebuilt and the Kinzies returned and were joined by about six families, the permanent residents of the area. For many years the Fort served as shelter for settlers moving West.

In 1827 Congress made a grant of land to aid in the construction of a canal which would connect the waters of Lake Michigan to the Illinois River. In 1829, when the State Legislature appointed a commission to mark out the route of the canal, and a surveyor appeared to mark out the town,

Chicago in 1818.

Chicago had, besides the garrison at Fort Dearborn, eight families, almost all in the Indian trade. In the Autumn of 1829 the commissioners authorized laying out the Town of Chicago. The first map of the town is dated August 4, 1830. This was the legal birth of Chicago, on an area covering about three-eighths of a square mile.

The canal had been eagerly sought for at least ten years. The first Governor of Illinois had called, at his inaugural in 1818, for the construction of a canal to connect Lake Michigan with the Illinois River, so that people could travel with their goods through the Great Lakes to the Mississippi and down to New Orleans. It was hoped that the prospective work on the canal would attract settlers to the town.

In 1832, when Biela's Comet reappeared and made its little tour of the Solar System, the tiny town was hit by a severe cholera epidemic. Nevertheless the first public religious services were held in that year in a log hut built to be used as a church. The tax list came to $148.29. A year later the settlement had increased enough to warrant its own post office and postmaster and a weekly delivery of mail. Late in 1833 a weekly newspaper, the *Chicago Democrat*, was started by John Calhoun.

On August 10, 1833, the voters of the town held an election to determine whether they should become incorporated into a city, and to elect trustees. Every man in the city voted: a total of twenty-eight voters, all males over the age of twenty-one. They decided upon incorporation.

In 1834 the number of voters increased to one hundred and eleven, and in 1835 it increased again, to two hundred and eleven. But the town's expansion was obviously not considered impressive: a request from Chicago to the State Bank for a loan of $25,000 was refused.

Finally, in 1837, the State Legislature approved incorporation of the City of Chicago and the following year William B. Ogden was elected the first Mayor. The total population of the City, at its inception, voters and non-voters combined, was 4,179.

Each year from 1840 to 1844 the population increased by one thousand people. In 1845 a surge occurred, and the City numbered twelve thousand souls, three times as many as it had when it was incorporated eight years earlier.

And the City was twenty-six years away from cosmic disaster.

3

Space on the Earth-Side of Jupiter, 1845

Biela's Comet moved smoothly along its ellipse: caught in Jupiter's gravitational embrace, it swung around that giant planet and went on toward the Sun. Its mass was somewhat less than it had been, since the tail generated on its last trip had been blown away by the solar wind. Now its head, rich with refrigerated dust, rock, gases and ice, began to glow as it absorbed solar energy; material from the misty shroud of the head swept back to form the tail once more, as it had on every journey to perihelion that the Comet had made.

On this journey in 1845, however, something unusual began to happen to Biela. More than a tail was sprouting from the Comet.

A bulge appeared at one side of the head, as though it were being ejected from it explosively. The eruption was being caused, most probably, by the action of the Comet's gases. The nucleus held methane and acetylene, both explosive gases, which may well have expanded with an uncontainable pressure. Whatever the reason, the Comet split into two parts, a greater and a lesser, each with a head and a tail. The new entity, impelled by the explosive force that gave it birth, soon took its own path, nearly parallel to the path of the mother Comet.

This action, taking place as it did hundreds of millions of miles from Earth, was of course not seen by astronomers who were awaiting Biela's return. On November 28, 1845, DeVico in Rome caught a fuzzy bit of light in his telescope. It was a first sighting of Biela's Comet. Two days later an astronomer in Berlin saw the tiny light. But the Comet was still too far away from Earth to be seen as anything more than a slowly moving patch of dim haze.

By the middle of December the Comet became more clearly visible, and the English astronomer Hind caught sight of it and noted that there was an unusual protuberance on one side of the nucleus. Finally, on January 13, 1846, Matthew Fontaine Maury in the U.S. Naval Observatory in Washington, D.C., definitely noted a double nucleus. Two days later Professor James Challis of Cambridge University noticed that the Comet had split into two distinct entities.

Challis, who has unfortunately become notorious for being the first observer to see the planet Neptune without recognizing that it was a planet, was distracted at the time by his search for the new planet, but he noted:

> On the evening of Jan 15, when I first sat down to observe it, I said to my assistant, "I see two comets." However, in altering the focus of the eyeglass and letting in a little illumination, the

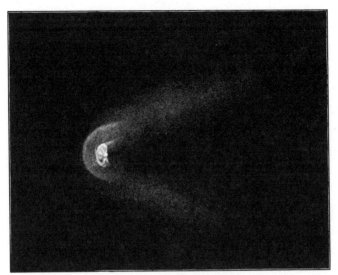

Head of Donati's Comet.

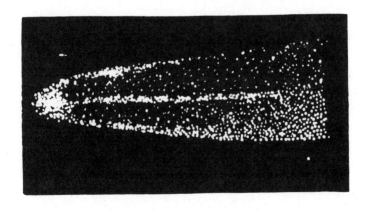

Bright-Centered Tail of Coggia's Comet, June, 1874.

smaller of the two comets appeared to resolve itself into a minute star with some haze about it. I observed the comet that evening but a short time, being in a hurry to proceed to observations of the new planet...

The next night he could not doubt his conclusion:

There are certainly two comets. The north preceding is less bright and of less apparent diameter than the other, and has a minute stellar nucleus... I think it can scarcely be doubted... that the two comets are not only apparently but really very near each other, and that they are physically connected. When I first saw the smaller, on 15 January, it was faint, and might easily have been overlooked. Now it is a very conspicuous object, and a telescope of moderate power will readily exhibit the most singular celestial phenomenon that has occurred for many years — a double comet.

Challis was quite overcome by the experience. "What can be the meaning of this?" he asked rhetorically. "Are they two independent comets? or is it a binary comet? or does my glass tell a false story? I incline to the opinion that it is a binary or double comet... But I never heard of such a thing..."

There were two comets following parallel paths through space. And difficult as it was to believe, there was a physical connection between them. Challis's observation was soon confirmed by others throughout the world. During the month of March in 1846, M.F. Maury saw an arc of light extending from the larger body to the smaller one, creating a kind of luminous bridge. The larger Comet appeared to have developed three tails, each at a one hundred and twenty degree angle to the next. This triple-tailed Comet was connected by an arc or bridge of light to a smaller one: it was the astronomical sight of a lifetime.

The comets had begun to separate, and the smaller one to grow much fainter than the large. By March 15 the small, faint comet could no longer be seen. And by April 22, neither Comet was visible.

The linked Comets rounded the Sun and made their way back to Jupiter. The explosive force that had ejected the small body from the large one continued to push the two Comets apart. The movement might be slight and slow, but the two had to have separate identities. They rushed through space together, following almost the same path that Biela's Comet had followed when it still contained within itself the material that was born as the smaller Comet.

It was almost the same path, but the laws of nature would not allow it to be the same path. Each body now traveled a slightly different course that would have to develop into an entirely different course over the passage of time.

In 1832 Biela I had passed within twenty thousand miles of Earth's orbit, one month before Earth itself had passed that point. Now the orbits of both Biela I and Biela II had changed slightly. Their approach to Earth's orbit would therefore change and the time of that approach would change as well.

No astronomer could calculate these changes even roughly. Whether they would be a matter of microseconds, months or years, and whether these new orbits would make their paths more, or less, likely to intersect with Earth's, would be decided by the inexorable laws of the cosmos.

4

Timber Country,
Wisconsin and Michigan, 1853

Most of the settlers in Wisconsin clustered close
to the southern end of Lake Michigan, near
Chicago. The northern part of the state, near
Green Bay, was sparsely settled. The winters
were severe there, and life was hard. Farmers
came, and cleared the land, which was fertile; but
clearing was a backbreaking job, since the area
was covered with immense forests, on either side
of the inland sea that was Lake Michigan.

Lumbermen and businessmen interested in
buying and selling lumber were attracted to
Wisconsin, which had become a state in 1848, and
also to Michigan which had joined the Union in
1837. There were maple, oak, beech, hemlock
and pine growing in incredible abundance: raw
material for housing and for railway ties to pull
together the young and sprawling nation.

David Jones had built a sawmill in 1836 at
Peshtigo on the west side of Green Bay in
Wisconsin, and then a few years later he had laid
out streets and offered lots for sale. The Bay was
there, extending southward like a thumb, there
were Lake Michigan and numerous rivers, all

offering good transport for the logs from the forests. But growth did not come as quickly as Jones had expected: by 1853 the country around Peshtigo had a total population of only four hundred and fifteen people.

The same thing was true across the Lake in Michigan, where the lumber center was at Saginaw on the Saginaw River. As in Wisconsin, small communities, made up largely of families from the East and of European immigrants, had sprung up around the sawmills. But most of the settlers were hardworking farmers. By 1866 there were only a few hundred families living in the northern forests on either side of Lake Michigan.

5

The Search for Biela, 1866

In September of 1852 Biela's Comet returned as expected, and was seen first by Pietro Angelo Secchi, an Italian astronomer. The two parts of the Comet were now separated by a distance of a million and a half miles. One Comet was a little ahead of the other. They were visible for over three weeks, and caused a considerable sensation. Only the discovery of Neptune in 1846 had caused a bigger sensation.

The two Comets were eagerly awaited on their expected return in May of 1859, but the astronomers were doomed to disappointment. The Comets traveled too close to the Sun for viewing, and consequently could not be seen. Their return was expected in 1865–66 when they would supposedly pass very close to the Earth; conditions for viewing would therefore be ideal. Astronomers began early to search for them; their predicted position had been worked out with great accuracy. There were now two distinct paths. But the Comets could not be seen.

Disappointment was rife at the meeting of the Royal Astronomical Society in England in the spring of 1866. The Comets had not been seen now for nearly fourteen years, and belief was growing that both Comets were dead. The same violent force which had created Biela II out of Biela I could have caused both Comets to break up into fragments. An astronomer named Talmage said at the Society meeting that he had seen a "cometic looking" sight on the fourth of November, 1865. He was experienced and respected, but a sighting like that could not be accepted on its face alone. The testimony of a less experienced astronomer, Buckingham, that he had made similar observations on November 9, 1865, was completely discounted. Searches were made at numerous European observatories but Continental astronomers had no more luck than English ones. Those who believed the Comets still existed consoled themselves with the thought that they would have another chance to see them in 1872.

6

Chicago, 1871

By 1866 Chicago had a population of two hundred thousand — nearly fifty times the population of 1836. It had become one of the largest cities in the country.

The people of the City were enterprising and filled with an aggressive self-confidence. In 1855 they had undertaken an ambitious but successful plan to make life in the City more comfortable; drainage had always been a public problem, since the land on which Chicago was built was only a few feet above the level of Lake Michigan. Consequently in rainy weather the streets and sidewalks became seas of mud, passable only at one's peril. So in the Winter of 1855 the City ordered the streets to be raised an average of eight to ten feet to relieve the problem of flooding.

The ground floors of the buildings would then as a consequence be several feet below street level. But, nothing daunted, the City fathers raised all buildings — brick, stone and wood — up to street level. All the large buildings — hotels, business blocks, warehouses — were raised by means of screws from their foundations to a

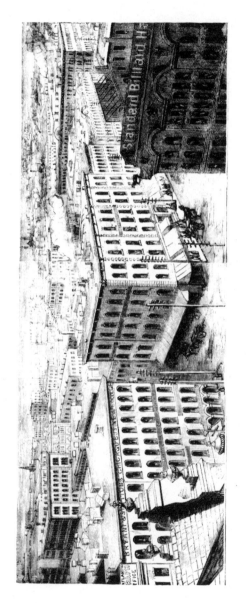

From the Courthouse, Looking South and Southeast.

height of six to ten feet, and new foundations were built under them. The harbor was dredged for the clay needed to fill the streets to the new grade and new plank sidewalks laid down.

This entailed a tremendous amount of inconvenience and expense over several years, but the people of the City undertook it with enthusiasm. And the results were gratifying. Deep dry cellars had been constructed and a new system of sewerage built. In 1866 the City had one hundred and sixty miles of sewer, as opposed to the six miles it had had in 1855 when the project started.

Another problem the City had faced was the quality of its water. In 1839 a company was chartered to supply the City's water. A reservoir was erected on the Lake shore at the corner of Michigan Avenue and Water Street. A pump with a small engine of twenty-five horsepower drew Lake water into the reservoir and distributed it through log pipes which had a bore of from three to five inches. In the fall of 1851 it was posited, to a good deal of ridicule, that by 1866 the City would have a population of one hundred thousand, and that a new water company must be formed.

A twenty by forty foot wooden crib was sunk six hundred feet out in the Lake. From this a wooden inlet was built through which water was carried to a large well, twenty-five feet deep. Over the well a pump was erected which, moved by a steam engine, forced the water into the mains. Large stone reservoirs were built at three points in the City, to accumulate water, which was then forced through the distributing pipes. A large tower surmounted the engine house: it was both a chimney for the boilers and a chamber for the standing column of water.

The water was first pumped in December, 1853, and first introduced into buildings in February, 1854.

While this was going on, immigrants were pouring into the City. There were three trunk lines of railroad from Chicago to the Atlantic seaboard and three West to the Mississippi. A road to the South had been built the entire length of the State. By 1860 there were more than one hundred and nine thousand people in Chicago and the beginning of the Civil War caused a further influx. Commerce on the River and in the harbor had grown immensely.

The City's sewage system, established along with the first water system, pushed all the sewage into the Chicago River. As the water was extended — by 1862 the length of water pipe was more than one hundred and five miles, still not sufficient — the water closets of all buildings were connected with the sewers. Large packing houses with cattle pens had been built on the River banks and its branches: all the refuse from them was emptied into the River.

As might be expected, the River became a cesspool, especially since it had no current except when the wind blew offshore. The smell was overpowering: whichever way the wind blew, a part of the City was assaulted by a fearful stench. When the wind blew offshore, the putrid stuff slowly seeped into the Lake, where it could be traced for miles by its inky color. When there were heavy rains the sickening water was carried away and for a few days the River was clean.

The smells of the Chicago River became legendary. The most horrible part of it, though, was that when the wind blew from the south or east, the River water which escaped into the Lake was carried up to the crib through which the water works obtained its water. It thus inevitably was distributed to the public. At times the homes of the populace reeked of this dreadful liquid. Not only was it black, with a shocking odor, but it was greasy to the touch. Something obviously had to be done.

In 1863 the City was authorized to construct a tunnel under the Lake to obtain a supply of pure water. After careful feasibility studies, and open bidding, ground was broken on March 17, 1864. A shore shaft was sunk twenty-six feet to the bottom of the sand bed. It was a cylinder nine feet in diameter inside and two and one quarter inches thick. From this shaft the tunnel was five feet wide and five feet two inches high, with semi-circular upper and lower arches. Bricks eight inches thick were laid lengthwise in two rings. The bottom of the tunnel where it connected with the Lake shaft was sixty-six feet below earth level and sixty-four feet below the level of the Lake. When the gate of the crib was closed, the tunnel emptied into the shore shaft and could be inspected and repaired, if necessary.

The work went on without a break, day and

Chicago Water Works.

night. A railroad was built in the tunnel and cars were filled with stiff blue clay and then drawn to the mouth by mules; the cars returned carrying bricks and cement. Nineteen months after the beginning of work at the shore end, in July, 1865, the monster crib which had been built for the Lake end of the tunnel was towed out into the Lake and sunk. It was an immense structure, forty feet high, and ninety-eight and one half feet in diameter. Inside it was a twenty-five foot space into which was fixed a nine foot round iron cylinder which extended sixty-four feet from the water line to the tunnel.

This structure, which contained seven hundred and fifty thousand feet of lumber, had to be firmly anchored so that it could not be dislodged by the incessant movement of the waters of the Lake. Its entire weight was five thousand seven hundred tons, and it stood twelve feet above the water line. As soon as it was anchored, a building was constructed over it to protect the workmen. Work on the tunnel began on the shore end in December, 1865, and was completed at both ends on the sixth of that month. In March, 1867, water was furnished to the City for the first time, and there was an impressive civic celebration.

To keep up with the increased water supply, the old engine and pumphouse were greatly enlarged. West of the pump, a new stone tower, one hundred and thirty feet high, was built. Inside the tower was an iron column three feet in diameter. Water was forced to the top of the column by the powerful pumping machine and then by its own pressure it was forced through the mains and distributing pipes of the City. The total cost of the whole work, including new engines, was about one million dollars — an astronomical sum in 1867.

The consumption of water in the City increased dramatically after these improvements were made. In 1866 the total amount averaged eight million, six hundred thousand gallons a day. In 1867, the first year that pure water was made available, it went up to eleven million, five hundred and sixty gallons daily. In 1869 it was about eighteen million, six hundred and thirty-three thousand, two hundred and seventy-eight, although on some days it went to twenty million gallons. By 1870 the average was twenty-one million gallons a day. The quality of the water was excellent, without sediment even in stormy weather.

The annual expenses of the water works, including salaries and repairs, were about eighty thousand dollars, and the cost of delivering the water per million gallons was less than ten thousand dollars. Annual income from water service was six hundred and fifty thousand dollars, which paid the interest on the water debt and left a surplus to pay for extension of the service pipes.

All this, of course, did not improve the condition of the River, which, except for the few months a year that it was coated with ice, poisoned the City's atmosphere. To offset this, the Illinois and Michigan Canal was fitted with a lock, the Canal being several feet above the River. Pumps were built to supply the Canal with water and the City used them to pump River water into the Canal continuously, and thus draw clean water into the River from the Lake. But as the population increased, the sewage in the River increased, and this method of pumping was too cumbersome and not efficacious. So the City received permission from the Legislature to deepen the Canal and establish a continuous flow of water upstream from the Lake, through the River into the Canal.

In June of 1871 this work was completed at a cost of three million, seven hundred and fifty thousand dollars. The locks were torn away, the River poured its inky stream of fetid water into the Canal and in twenty-four hours the River water was as clean as the Lake. A current flowed constantly at several miles an hour to the head of the stream, keeping the River pure. The Chicago River had been forced to flow backwards: a modern engineering miracle.

In the thirty-four years since its incorporation the City had become the leading grain market of the world, a major port and a railroad center. It had twenty-five banks, seventeen of them national, large hotels, an opera house, parks and boulevards.

An article in *The Chicago Tribune* for the fifth of October, 1871, detailed improvements in trade for the city's merchants. The main point of the article was that the Treasury Department had granted permission to shippers to carry foreign

Drake and Farwell Block, Wabash Avenue.

Illinois and Michigan Central Railroad Depot.

goods on which there was no duty, in the same bonded cars with goods on which duty had to be paid:

Few persons, except those directly engaged in the import trade of this city, are aware of what important changes have resulted from the recent removal of the unnecessary restrictions in regard to cars, and locks, and guards, that were imposed a year ago upon the shipment of goods direct from foreign ports to this city.

Leading dealers in dry goods, ribbons, hosiery, carpets, liquors, crockery, and other imported items announced to the *Tribune* that they were importing five to six times as much as they had at the same season a year earlier. In addition, Chicago merchants were now employing their own exclusive agents in Europe:

Now, at least four prominent houses keep either members of firms or an exclusive agent in Europe, the greater portion of the year, moving from one market to another, now buying German cloths, now at Basle for ribbons and hosiery, and again in England for carpets, etc. During the last four weeks, a thousand tons of railroad iron have been received in Chicago, direct from England via Montreal, and we hear of another thousand tons afloat for here, that will arrive within the next few weeks.

Chicago merchants were buying six times more of their goods direct from foreign manufacturers and cutting out middlemen in New York and other cities in the Eastern United States:

As far as direct trade with Europe is concerned, this great change has been effected by relieving the Chicago importing merchant from the necessity of doing his warehousing in New York City instead of at home. The Chicago merchant now pays nothing until his goods arrive here, he gives his bond here, the goods are appraised here, and he can withdraw any portion of them from warehouse on any day and have them in his store without further delays.

Thus the demand for Government bonded warehouse room in the City had increased so much that the Michigan Southern Company was now building a bonded warehouse on Harrison Street, and that company, along with others in New York, intended to bond their lines in order to make a specialty of carrying goods imported directly to Chicago.

In addition, the *Tribune* pointed out proudly, it was not just with Europe that direct trade had increased that fall. The tea trade had increased even more than the dry goods trade:

It is a fact of great significance... that whereas the total quantity of teas in Government bonded warehouses in this city, on September 30, 1870, was only 2,500 chests, it is now nearly 15,000 chests, all of which has come direct on through bills of lading from Hong Kong and Yokohama, through San Francisco to Chicago, without a day's unnecessary delay, and there are further receipts of teas now via the North Western and Rock Island Railroads every day.

This great increase in direct importing had

come mainly in the last two months; the amount of duties paid during September of that year were over three times as great as during the same time the year before.

As regards the tea trade, there seems no reason why Chicago will not become the great distributing market for all the central parts of the continent between the Allegheny and the Rocky Mountains...

The trans-continental railroad on the one hand, and the increased facilities for direct importation on the other, are revolutionizing the foreign trade of the United States.

Obviously, Chicago was anxious to take its place among the great cities of the world. It made up in energy for what it lacked in years. Its rise into world prominence had been meteoric. It was brash and boastful, and surely no one expected that any force from outside it could slow its progress or divert its citizens from their intense preoccupations with their goals.

7

Chicago and the Lake Regions
Saturday, October 7, 1871

The Fall of 1871 was an unusually dry one in
the Midwest, following an unusually dry summer. Prairie fires were burning; in themselves
these fires were not alarming, since they were
common in the autumn. Even when they spread
to the woods, people were not disturbed about
them, since much of the timber in the woods was
green — even in an autumn as dry as the autumn
of 1871. But in this autumn prairie fires were
burning over wider areas than anyone could
remember before.

In the area around Green Bay, Wisconsin,
where a railroad was being built, it had been
expected that the swampy ground would cause
problems for the workers. But the swamps had
dried up; the ground was firm under the picks
of the railway workers. In some areas which had
been swampy the previous spring, it had been
necessary for the men to dig down ten feet to find
water at all.

A few residents were forced to leave their
homes because of the small fires which kept
breaking out in the forests of Wisconsin and

Michigan, but most people accepted these fires as normal Midwest autumn phenomena.

In Chicago all through the summer and fall it had been unusually hot with no measurable rain. High southwest winds had been blowing for weeks, parching the prairies and all the timber inside and outside the City. During the first week of October there had been a succession of small fires in the City, but these had been quickly and efficiently dealt with by the Fire Department.

On Saturday, October 7, a blaze broke out in the basement of Lull and Holmes' planing mill on South Canal Street and spread quickly to a paper-box factory, lumberyards and the omni-present cottages made of pine. The wind was high, and four blocks burned, bounded by Van Buren and Adams, Clinton Street and the south branch of the Chicago River. The firemen had to make every effort to prevent the fire from spreading through the West Side. Many of these men had been on duty for seventy-two hours without relief. The Sunday morning papers referred to this fire as "The Great Conflagration": it was the largest fire which had ever struck Chicago. Sixteen acres were gutted, a hundred families lost their homes, and piles of coal and lumber in the yards on the banks of the River had been wiped out. But no one had been killed, and the excellent water system had served the exhausted firemen well.

There was no danger from that fire and there seemed to be no danger from the fires in Wisconsin and Michigan. But a danger did exist.

Some two million miles away a dark body, small by cosmic standards but immense by earthly standards, was hurtling along an elliptical path directly toward Earth at thirty miles a second. It was on a collision course.

Gale's Comet, May 5, 1894.

8

Sunday, October 8, 1871
Space

Biela's Comet, which was expected to return in 1872, had not been clearly sighted since 1852. Since it had first been seen by Wilhelm von Biela, and charted by astronomers, it had become two Comets instead of one. Neither of these two could have the same orbit and the same speed that Biela's Comet would have had when it was alone. Since one of Nature's basic laws is that to every action there is an equal and opposite reaction, both Biela I and Biela II had to follow new paths.

In 1852, they had been observed to be drifting apart. Since then no one had been able to observe them long enough to tell whether either or both had slowed their pace or were moving more rapidly. No one could be certain about the periods of either of the two Comets.

Let us assume that Biela II had an orbit which was carrying it farther and farther from Biela I. The impact of its creation might have slowed its speed and its new ellipse might not carry it past Jupiter's orbit, the route that Biela I took. Let us assume that while Biela Major was still moving to the outermost point of its ellipse, Biela Minor had already reached that point in its new orbit. Assume that while the major Comet was moving back away from the Sun on its way to aphelion, past Jupiter, the ejected segment had already reached aphelion and was now falling back toward the Sun.

If that were the case, then on the night of October 8, 1871, around 9:30 P.M. Central Standard time, while Biela I was still a year away from its crossing of Earth's orbit, Biela II could be on an infinitesimally different course. Since a miniscule difference is significant in spatial terms, Biela II could at that moment be crossing the orbit of Earth.

The infinitesimal difference in speed could bring Biela II to Earth's vicinity a year sooner than the time charted for Biela I. And the course could be shifted so that it would not pass Earth's orbit a month after Earth itself reached that same point in space. Thus it would not miss Earth itself by twenty thousand miles as Biela I did in 1832: it would instead have been heading straight for Earth. It could actually cross Earth's orbit, coming from the north, just as Earth itself was moving eastward through that same point in space.

If that were to have happened, then the fires in that small part of North America surrounding the Great Lakes could almost have seemed like a kind of beacon, guiding a rapidly moving celestial body toward its terrestrial target.

A comet is not really a unified object. It is thought to consist of motes of dust, grains of sand,

Naked-Eye View of Donati's Comet, October 4, 1858.

and bits of gravel, encased in a slushy frame made up of frozen water and gases. The nucleus of any comet may be a relatively small portion of rock: the eruption that produced Biela II may not have provided a nucleus for it. In that case Biela II would have been composed only of frozen gases, water and clusters of gravel and sand. Other fragments erupted at the moment of its birth could well have been lost amid the jetsam of the Solar System.

Let us assume that Biela II consisted of three parts in a loosely compacted cluster, and that these were moving though space like an arrowhead flying backward.

The base of the arrow would necessarily lead the way, with its corners one hundred miles apart. The apex of the triangle that was the arrowhead would lie some two hundred miles behind each corner of its base.

Among the gases that comets contain are methane and acetylene. In the vacuum of space these gases glow when they are bombarded by solar energy: thus the comets are luminous. On Earth, methane and acetylene burn in the presence of oxygen; they can produce temperatures in excess of six thousand degrees Fahrenheit. Methane burns at twelve hundred degrees Fahrenheit, double the kindling point of wood. These gases remain inert, of course, in the eternal coldness of space, where they are capable of interacting slowly with other cosmic materials. But when the comet nears the Sun, more violent reactions could possibly occur in these gases.

Such a reaction may well have caused the birth of Biela II.

This baby Comet could not contain enough gases to be affected by the Sun: it is a dim Comet; it does not even glow. But we may ask ourselves what would happen if those gases which Biela II must contain were to be released into an atmosphere rich in oxygen, in which fires were already burning?

On that Sunday night in 1871 the North American continent, seen from space on the blue planet of Earth, would have been in shadow, with glimmerings of fire piercing the pall of smoke over the area of the Great Lakes around Lake Michigan. If, out of the blackness of space, a small Comet hurtled, caught up in Earth's orbit; if that Comet hit the Earth from the east, head-on, then friction with the atmosphere could have quickly ignited the gases which made up a large part of the comet, destroying them and turning the sand and gravel components of the body into sparks which would glow brightly for an instant before being transformed into ashes.

But if that Comet came from the north, it would plunge into the atmosphere of Earth at only twelve miles a second. The blanket of air which surrounds the Earth would slow the movement of the Comet and cause its temperature, which would be near the absolute zero of space, to rise. As the body's plunge continued through the atmosphere, the icy slush would melt.

When the Comet struck the Earth, its gases

would thus be freed. Its two forward masses, the corners of the base of the triangle, would strike first on either side of Lake Michigan, and halfway up its length. Then, still moving at the speed of lightning, the single body that was the triangle's trailing apex would catch up with the forward masses and pass them, to strike the Earth an instant later, a few hundred miles to the south.

If this were to happen, three points on the Earth would flare up and the three bodies, three parts of one dead Comet, would come violently to life, transmuted into three gigantic fire bombs. In Chicago, in Wisconsin around the Peshtigo area, in Michigan around Manistee, the gases would fuel fires that could not be brought under control because they would be extraterrestrial fires, burning with a power and heat outside the experience of men.

9

Chicago
Sunday, October 8, 1871
9:30 P.M.

The eighth of October, 1871, was a very sultry Sunday in Chicago. The population had gone about its usual business that day: Sunday dinners, church and family visits. Suddenly, about half past nine o'clock in the evening, the fire-bells began once more to clang. Many people believed that a fire had broken out in a barn about forty feet from the house of Patrick O'Leary at No. 112 De Koven Street, east of Jefferson, although even then there were some who said it did not start there at all, but in the rear of the Old Armory, which was across the street from the outbuildings of the Gas Works.

One eyewitness who went immediately to the O'Leary's neighborhood was Joseph Edgar Chamberlain, a reporter on the *Chicago Evening Post*. He was on the scene in a few minutes. He said:

> The fire had already advanced a distance of about a single square block through the frame buildings that covered the ground thickly north

of De Koven Street and east of Jefferson Street —
if those miserable alleys shall be dignified by
being denominated streets. That neighborhood
had always been a *terra incognita* to respectable
Chicagoans, and during a residence of three
years in the city I had never visited it. The land
was thickly studded with one-story frame
dwellings, cow stables, pigsties, corn-cribs, sheds
innumerable; every wretched building within
four feet of its neighbor, and everything of wood
— not a brick or a stone in the whole area.

Other people left their memories of that
Sunday evening on paper.

Mr. Alexander Frear, a member of the New
York State Assembly, told a reporter for *The
New York World* that on Sunday night, October
8, he had gone to the Sherman House at his
sister's request to see if some friends of hers had
arrived from Milwaukee. The hotel was crowded, as usual, with people from out of town and
with Chicago businessmen. People filled the
corridors and parlors, chatting and killing time.
While Mr. Frear was looking through the hotel
register for the names of his sister's friends,
someone said, "There go the fire-bells again."
Someone else responded jocosely, "They'll burn
the city down if they keep on." Mr. Frear paid
little attention to this, because he did not find
it interesting. The names he wanted were not on
the register.

He was not particularly anxious to go home, so
he sauntered for a while through the hotel corridors until he met someone he knew: a Mr. Nixon,

who had an upholstery shop on Lake Street. Mr. Frear settled down for a chat. "Look," Mr. Nixon said, "there goes George Francis Train." "No," Mr. Frear said, "I know Train very well, that's not Train." While they were discussing this, Mr. Frear's eighteen-year-old nephew came up to him. Mr. Frear appealed to him: was that Train or wasn't it? The nephew was not interested in Mr. Train. He told the two men that a big fire was burning on the West Side. Mr. Frear, still bored by fire talk, asked the boy to walk over to Ewing Street and tell his sister that her friends had not arrived. But his nephew said Mr. Frear had better go himself, because the fire was in that vicinity, and he himself had a friend waiting for him upstairs.

Mr. Frear parted with Mr. Nixon and left the hotel. The wind was blowing fiercely through Clark Street to the River and he had some difficulty in getting across Courthouse Square. He recalled later that it could not yet have been ten o'clock when he left the hotel, because as he passed Follansbee's Bank he heard singing in the Methodist Church. He noticed the glare of the fire on the West Side, but he was still not interested in it.

There were few people on the streets. He met no one until at Monroe Street he saw a policeman walking rapidly toward him. Mr. Frear asked him politely if he knew anything about the fire; the policeman looked at him without answering and hurried on. This struck Mr. Frear as odd. He saw a small group of men standing on the corner

Sherman House.

Field, Leiter & Co.'s Building,
Corner of State and Washington Streets.

of Adams Street and he stopped to ask them the same question. One of them said, "It must be a damn big fire this time; you can't put out a high wind with water." The rest of them were silent, and Mr. Frear thought they looked a little scared. While he stood there, feeling strangely unwilling to walk on, a policeman came up Adams Street on horseback and turned onto Clark Street. Some of the men hallooed to him, but he paid no attention to them. Mr. Frear, now distinctly nervous, resumed his walk but before he reached the next street cinders began to fall thick and fast all around him. It was growing lighter all the time.

A great many people could now be seen looking out of their windows, and the streets suddenly seemed to fill with people. They were not excited. They stood about in groups listening to the wind. It was making a noise very like the Lake on a stormy night.

Mr. Frear saw that the door to a Dutch beer-saloon was half open, and he decided to go in and get a cigar: a normal action during an evening's walk. The gas was burning, but the people who kept the place were all out on the street. Mr. Frear helped himself to a cigar from an open box that was standing on the counter and lit it at the gas burner. He left the saloon without being stopped. While he was holding the cigar to the gas jet he noticed for the first time that he was considerably excited himself; his hand was shaking and he could hear his heart beat. He was sure he had not been in the place for two minutes, but when he came out cinders were falling like snowflakes in every direction, the street was extremely bright and there was "a great hubbub of men and vehicles."

Now thoroughly alarmed, he began to run toward Van Buren Street, but the walks were so crowded with people and the cinders were blowing so fast and so thickly that he could not get through. In addition, the wind blew his hat off twice. He took to the middle of the street and found that the crowd coming from the opposite direction was increasing. But it was difficult to see anything on account of the cinders.

Somewhere between Van Buren and Polk Streets he found that the crowd was jammed "solidly" in the street. On the east side of the street was a four-story brick house, taller than all the others around it. A man stood on the roof gesticulating and shouting. Mr. Frear thought he was shouting to the crowd, but his voice was lost in the wind. It was some time before Mr. Frear made out that the man was shouting to someone in a window below him, and that man was repeating his words to the crowd. All Mr. Frear could hear distinctly were the words, "Burning on both sides of the River." Just then the people in the street began to fall back: a man on horseback was forcing his way through. Mr. Frear thought he looked like a gentleman and took him for an insurance officer. He was waving a little red flag like the one railway switchmen used, from side to side. Mr. Frear could not hear his words, but they seemed to produce panic in the crowd.

Mr. Frear now understood that it was

impossible and dangerous to go on the way he was going and he turned around, intending to run to the first bridge he saw. But then he saw that the light of the fire extended far back in the direction from which he had just come: flames were lighting the houses on the east side of Clark Street as far as he could see. He began to run as fast as he could go to the Adams Street bridge. Vehicles and people on foot were streaming in from all streets to the West. Mr. Frear was now extremely anxious to get to his sister's house.

He fought his way to the bridge. It was filled with teams of horses vying to cross it, while tugs stood in the water screaming their intention to get through. There was a rush of people toward Mr. Frear, who realized that the bridge was going to be raised; he ran to get over. A woman carrying a bureau drawer, and blinded by the sparks and cinders, in her desperation struck him in the chest with the drawer. He was stunned for a moment with the pain, and then he took out his watch, and discovered that she had broken the crystal. It was now 11:30. While he held his watch in his hand a live coal fell on it, as large as a silver dollar.

All of Adams Street reaching to Des Plaines on the West Side was choked with people, but the terrible rain of cinders had stopped at that location; it was being carried by the wind in a northeasterly direction across the River. Des Plaines Street was comparatively clear. While he was running into it, Mr. Frear lost his hat again. This time he did not bother to attempt to retrieve

it but went on running as fast as he could go in
the direction of Ewing Street.

Joseph Edgar Chamberlain was in Ewing
Street that night. He watched the firemen fight-
ing the flames, "stupidly and listlessly," he said,
because they had worked hard all Saturday
night and most of Sunday night and were "ener-
vated" by the whisky which flowed freely on
such occasions. As Chamberlain stepped in
among some sheds south of Ewing Street, a fence
next to him burst into flames. He moved hastily
away, and in five minutes the spot where he had
been standing became engulfed in fire.

Ewing Street, he said, was a much-used
thoroughfare for the area. It was really nothing
more than an alley but nonetheless it was broader
than the surrounding streets. Everybody was
saying that when the fire reached a wide
boulevard, it would burn itself out. It was on
Ewing Street, which had elevated wooden
sidewalks and was wide enough for teams to pass
each other in dry weather, that, Chamberlain
noted, "the real panic began." People were
pouring out of the thickly-settled area between
Jefferson Street and the River: the "wretched
female inhabitants" who were almost naked,
were begging people to help them with their
quilts, cane-bottomed chairs and iron kettles.
Drays thundered past, adding to the confusion.

Chamberlain moved on to Harrison Street,
since this was a wide boulevard, and it was hoped
it would stop the fire. But "the same scene of
hurry and confusion was repeated at Harrison on

Bookseller's Row, State Street.

Clark Street, South from Washington Street.

a larger scale than at Ewing; and that same scene kept on increasing in terror all night long as the fire moved northward." The universal remark among the crowd was, "If it passes this, nothing can stop it but last night's burned district." The fire reached Harrison Street and broke out "almost simultaneously" for a distance of two blocks. The two fire engines which had been standing in the street "fled in terror." The wind drove burning brands into the houses on the north side of the street. These were made of brick, but nonetheless they ignited like tinder and the fire swept on to the north.

When Chamberlain reached Van Buren Street, the southern limit of the Saturday night fire, the words "Across the River," were passing through the crowd. People were incredulous; no one could believe that the fire had passed over the River. Chamberlain went with the others, seeking confirmation of the rumor. When they reached what once had been Canal Street, they could see, through clouds of smoke, a bright light across the River:

> I rushed to the Adams Street viaduct and across the bridge. The Armory, the Gas Works, "Conley's Patch" and Wells Street as far north as Monroe were all on fire. The wind had increased to a tempest and hurled great blazing brands over our heads.
>
> At this point my duty called me to my home in the West Division; but within an hour I was back again to witness the doom of the blazing city, of which I then had a full presentiment. The streets

on the West Side were as light as broad noon. I
looked at my watch and saw it was just two
o'clock. As I ran down Monroe Street, with the
burning town before me, I contemplated the ruin
that was working, and the tears rose to my eyes
... I choked down the tears, and they did not rise
again that night.

At one o'clock in the afternoon on Monday,
when most of the City lay in ruins, the only
downtown newspaper which appeared was *The
Evening-Journal-Extra*, and here Mrs. O'Leary's
cow made her first appearance.

> The fire broke out [the *Journal* said] on the
> corner of De Koven and Twelfth streets, at about
> nine o'clock on Sunday evening, being caused by
> a cow kicking over a lamp in a stable in which a
> woman was milking. An alarm was immediately
> given, but, owing to the high southwest wind,
> the building was speedily consumed, and thence
> the fire spread rapidly...

It should be noted that the O'Learys lived on
De Koven and Jefferson Streets, and not Twelfth
Street, and that in this first appearance of The
Cow, Mrs. O'Leary was present in the barn at
the time. Nine days later, on October 18, the
Chicago Times picked up the theme with vari-
ations:

> Flames were discovered in a small stable to the
> rear of a house on the corner of De Koven and
> Jefferson streets. Living at the place indicated
> was an old Irish woman... On the morning of the
> fire she was found by a reporter for the *Times*
> sitting on the front steps of her own house... At

first she refused to speak one word about the fire, but only screamed at the top of her voice, 'My poor cow, my poor cow! She is gone and I have nothing left in the world.' Finally she was induced to talk... It had been her regular nightly habit to visit the stable and see if her cow was all right. On Sunday night about 9½ o'clock she took a lamp in her hands and went out to have a look at her pet. Then she took a notion the cow must have some salt, and she set down the lamp and went in the house for some. In a moment the cow had accidentally kicked over the lamp, an explosion followed and in an instant the structure was enveloped in flames.

Mrs. O'Leary was actually sitting on her own front steps, a remarkable achievement when her street was supposedly the first to go in the incredible firestorm. Here again the fire apparently broke out not in Mrs. O'Leary's presence, but while she walked in the dark back to her house, leaving the lighted lamp with the cow.

Still another version of the story surfaced from a Mr. S.H. Kimball who lived at the time of the fire near the corner of Washington and Lincoln Streets on the West Side. Mr. Kimball deposited a document with the Chicago Historical Society in which he said that he had gone to look for mementoes of the fire on Tuesday morning and was driven away by Mrs. O'Leary who was wielding a broomstick. Undaunted he slipped back when she was not looking and found what he believed to be a piece of the original lamp that started the fire!

Later, his family hired an Irish cook who became very much excited when he showed her the piece of lamp and told him she could tell him how the fire started, but he must keep it a secret:

It seems she lived in the vicinity of the O'Leary house and knew the O'Learys. She also had a family of friends living near the O'Learys. She made the statement to me that a lot of young people were having a dance the night the fire started. They wanted to make a little punch but were out of milk, and someone suggested they go over and milk Mrs. O'Leary's cow. They picked up a glass lamp... and went to the shed, and, while attempting to milk the cow, the lamp was kicked over and they fled.

I showed her the piece of lamp, and she said she was very positive that it was the style of lamp that they had in their house. She seemed greatly excited about the matter and got my promise that I would say nothing about it for fear these people should get into trouble. A very short time after that she left the house without giving any warning, and we were never able to locate her. Soon after she left I found that this piece of lamp had disappeared.

These stories, varying as they do, and carrying the unmistakeable tinge of the anti-Irish sentiment of the period, are almost certainly apocryphal. Mrs. O'Leary's cow was not accepted as the cause of the fire at the time. Mabel McIlvaine wrote caustically:

The cow, the lamp and the bowl of punch have been made much of in Chicago for reasons of our own. The fact that we had fifty-six miles of wooden-block pavement, and six hundred and fifty-one miles of wooden sidewalks might have seemed too much like "preparedness." And the other facts of our having but one pumping-station in the whole city, and that roofed with wood, together with our fourteen fire-engines among some three hundred thousand inhabitants — these things are too inconvenient to discuss. Then, too, our custom of allowing landlords to erect wooden cottages in the immediate vicinity of gas works, and at the approaches to bridges and tunnels — well, we knew better but we did not like to be militant.

Mr. Kimball's Irishwoman need not have been agitated about Mr. Kimball keeping her guilty secret, since Mrs. O'Leary's name had already appeared in the *Evening Journal* and, in fact, an official inquiry into the origin and progress of the fire was held in Chicago in the fall of 1871 and Mrs. O'Leary, along with her husband and friends were called to testify.

Mrs. O'Leary said that she, her husband and five children, were in bed, but not yet asleep on that Sunday night and they knew nothing about a fire until Mr. Sullivan, a neighbor, called them and said that their barn was on fire. When Mrs. O'Leary looked at the barn it was already ablaze — as were two other barns as well. She said she "became almost crazy" because she knew she was going to lose all her stock: in addition to the barn, wagons and harness, she owned six cows and a horse, all of which perished in the fire. A family named McLaughlin rented the front of the house from the O'Learys, and Mrs. O'Leary had heard that they were having a "social time" on that Sunday night: they had an oyster supper and a Mrs. White had told her that one of that family went into the barn to milk one of the cows. She knew nothing about it herself. She first saw a fire engine working on Turner's Block, on the corner of Jefferson and De Koven streets. She was so upset looking after her family and her property that she could not notice anything else.

Her husband Patrick said that he had been in bed and knew nothing about the start of the fire. When he saw it, only his barn was ablaze. He had no knowledge of how the fire started. His "woman" went to bed about eight o'clock and he followed her half an hour afterward. "If he was to be hanged for it" he couldn't tell how the fire started, and "he didn't blame any man in America for it."

Catharine McLaughlin, who rented the front of the O'Leary house, also testified that she knew nothing about the origin of the fire. Someone cried "Fire!" and she looked around the side of the house and saw O'Leary's barn burning and the rear of Mr. Dalton's house just igniting. There were five young men and two young women at her house that night, her friends and cousins who had come in to see a "greenhorn" cousin of hers who had just arrived from Ireland. Her husband — Pat McLaughlin, the fiddler — played two tunes on his fiddle, and one of the women danced a "bout" and another a polka. That was all the dancing they did that night.

One of the company went out once or twice during the evening and brought in half a gallon of beer. They didn't eat anything and she didn't cook anything — she did not start the stove. "Before God, this day," she didn't cook anything. The company was in the house when the fire broke out. She did not know whether Mrs. O'Leary was in the habit of milking her cows at night; she knew she milked them generally about five o'clock. The barn was about forty feet from the house, but since she lived in the front of the house, she said the barn could have been turned upside down and she wouldn't have known it.

None of the company, she said emphatically, went out to get milk for punch. She never had such a thing in the house.

Catharine Sullivan, whose husband woke the O'Learys, and who lived on De Koven Street, east of Jefferson, was washing dishes when she saw a bright reflection on the window panes of her dwelling. She ran into the street and saw that O'Leary's barn and two others east of it were on fire. Her son and Dennis Rogan woke the O'Learys. She did not know of her own knowledge that there was a party at the O'Leary's but she had heard that there was.

Dennis Rogan of 112 De Koven Street was in the O'Leary house about half-past eight on that Sunday night. O'Leary and his wife had gone to bed; Mrs. O'Leary had a sore foot. He went home too and went to bed about nine o'clock. He heard someone say that O'Leary's barn was on fire.

He ran out to try and save a wagon he saw there, but the heat drove him away. He knew there was company at McLaughlin's because he heard music in there, but he did not know who was there. He thought it took about fifteen minutes before the engines came. There was a high wind, and sparks were blowing some distance away.

Daniel Sullivan, of No. 134 De Koven Street, was in O'Leary's house about eight o'clock in the evening and remained there about one hour. O'Leary and three of his children left early to go to bed; Mrs. O'Leary left too, saying she did not feel well. Just before Sullivan left, Mr. O'Leary came back and told the other two children to go to bed.

At about twenty minutes past nine, from his house across the street, Sullivan saw the fire in O'Leary's barn. He hobbled across the street — he had a wooden leg — crying "Fire!" and went into the barn. His mother kept a cow and he frequently went to O'Leary's barn to get feed, so he knew how the cows were tied. He cut two of them loose, but they balked at leaving. The fire was getting worse, so he decided to leave but, as he was making for the door, his wooden leg caught between two boards. He fell over, catching himself on his sound leg, caught hold of the wall and, pulling himself up, noticed a calf tied up near him. The hair on its back was on fire. When he caught hold of the rope, the calf leaped six feet in the air. He pulled it out of the barn and looked back, when he reached the yard, feeling like a "whipped dog" because he hadn't saved the cows. By this time the O'Leary's barn was on fire, and a man named Rogan pushed in their door and woke them. It took ten to fifteen minutes for the engines to arrive; two barns were on fire when they came. There might have been more, but he could only remember two. The fire did not spread very rapidly.

From the foregoing testimony, at least one citizen concluded that "it was quite evident that a drunken orgy of some description was going on, which undoubtedly had much to do with the more immediate cause of the fire." This was unquestionably because the inhabitants of the houses on De Koven Street were Irish and poor; obviously the "orgy" could not have lasted more than an hour or two, since most people left before nine o'clock, children were present, and somebody brought in some beer, not the strongest nor the quickest-acting intoxicant in existence.

Fire Marshal Williams testified that the fire in the O'Leary's barn was put firmly under control and could not have gone a foot farther. But he said, the next thing he knew, they came and told him that St. Paul's church, about two blocks north, was on fire. To the Fire Marshal it did not appear possible that the O'Leary barn could have been responsible for this fire, which skipped and leaped about in so freakish a way.

Marshal Williams said he told George Raw, the foreman of Hook and Ladder #2, to put his longest ladder on the truck and go to St. Paul's church, because he knew the wind was blowing so hard they couldn't raise a stream high enough to strike the roof. "Citizens," however — either in a playful or hysterical frame of mind — got hold of the ladder, threw it down, and broke it in half.

Nevertheless the church fire was surrounded: three engines were working on it. At Clinton and Mather streets it was so hot that the engineer had to set up a door to protect himself. Another engine, called the Gund, was on the east side of the church and a third, the Coventry, was on the north.

The fire was checked. It did not gain any headway because the church fell in. There was a drug store on the opposite side of the street — the northwest corner, and a row of buildings north of it, and these caught fire several times. They held the fire at bay, and the next thing Williams knew, the fire was in Bateham's planing mill.

For the second time, the fire, which the men had thought was coming under control, leapt suddenly to a new area. Williams rushed to the planing mill. When he got there he discovered the match factory between Bateham's and Clinton Street was going, along with the lumber in a nearby yard just north of it. They got two streams in there, but the fire was too thick and heavy for them to do any good. It ran along north to another lumberyard and then spread east to the old red mill.

The Marshal went north to head it off, and found it was down to Harrison Street. The Fire Commissioner came up, considerably upset and said to Williams, "Don't you know the fire is ahead of you?" Williams told him that it was getting ahead of him in spite of all he could do; it was just driving him right along.

Williams got down to Van Buren Street and was working the engines there, but it was so hot that the men had to run for their lives, leaving their hose behind on the ground. They came to Williams and asked him what they should do about hose. "God only knows," Williams said.

While the unnerved citizens of Chicago were attempting to cope with an uprecedented catastrophe, two more catastrophes were taking place two hundred miles to the north.

10

Wisconsin, Green Bay Area
Sunday, October 8, 1871
9:30 P.M.

Throughout this unusually dry autumn there had been the usual prairie fires which had been fought off with the usual zeal. In Peshtigo, the small community on the west bank of Green Bay, people spent their Sunday at peace, at least as far as their immediate well-being was concerned. They lived in a most beautiful area: Peshtigo lay on both sides of the Peshtigo River, and covered about one square mile. It had been thirty-five years since the first sawmill had been built at Peshtigo; by 1871 the village had a total population of about one thousand four hundred. Five hundred people worked at the Peshtigo Company, which consisted of the largest tub and pail factory in the United States, a machine shop, and foundry, and saw, planing and flour mills.

At sundown the strong winds which had been blowing for days suddenly stopped. There was a noticeable lull, a quiet which lasted for over two hours. It seemed like a peaceful autumn Sabbath evening.

At a few minutes past nine — about the time of the first outburst of the Chicago Fire — the people of the village heard a terrible roar. It seemed to be a tornado crashing through the forests. Instantly the sky, which had been dark a moment before, was illumined with a terrible glare: it seemed to have burst into clouds of flame. A spectator said later that the fire did not come upon them gradually from burning trees and other objects to the windward, but the first notice they had of it was a whirlwind of flame in great clouds from above the tops of trees, which fell and entirely enveloped everything. The people who inhaled the intensely hot air dropped dead.

Corpses were later found in the roads and fields: there was no visible mark of a fire any-where near them, and their bodies and clothing were not burnt in any way. But they were un-deniably dead. At the Sugar Bush, an extended clearing four miles wide in some places, corpses were found in the open road between fences which were lightly scorched. There was no mark of fire upon these people; they lay as if they were asleep. Many were killed in compact masses. They seemed to have huddled together in what they thought were the safest places, away from buildings, trees and other inflammable material, and to have died there together. Fences around cleared fields were burned in spots of only a few rods in length, and elsewhere not touched at all. Fish were killed as they swam in the streams.

Great clouds of fire had fallen out of the sky

and enveloped everything in Peshtigo, and not just in Peshtigo. The track of what was later called "the great Sunday night tornado" started, on the west side, about six miles north of Oconto: it was fifteen miles wide and parallel thirty miles northward down the Bay. On the east side the track started in the town of Humboldt and ranged ten miles wide, sweeping northeast forty miles to Big Sturgeon Bay. The west district took in, in addition to Peshtigo, the Sugar Bush Settlement, the village of Menekaune at the mouth of the Menominee, and the Birch Creek Settlement, eight miles inside the Michigan border. All were swept out of existence.

And east, across Lake Michigan, another fiery catastrophe started at the same moment.

Michigan, too, had suffered from fires during that dry autumn. In Manistee, a town to the east of Peshtigo across Lake Michigan, which was connected to Lake Michigan by Lake Manistee, a fire broke out that Sunday at nine in the morning. There was a strong wind. The firemen worked all day, and were relieved to see that, despite the wind, the fire did not spread. It was extinguished, but as darkness fell the citizens saw a glow in the sky to the west, coming from the shore of Lake Michigan, where the pine woods there had caught fire.

Then at 9:30 P.M., the same time that fire broke out in Chicago and in the area around Peshtigo, Wisconsin, the fire alarm sounded again. To their horror, the people of Manistee saw a bright red glare in the western sky near the mouth of the Manistee River. This was a fire of a new character, out of control. They wondered what was happening.

Perhaps the answer lay in the heavens.

11

Michigan and Wisconsin Both Sides of Lake Michigan Sunday Night, October 8, 1871

When the fire alarm sounded in Manistee, Michigan, the fire fighters rushed toward the mouth of the Manistee River where the western sky was glowing red. There were a large mill, a boarding house and several homes — about twenty-five or thirty — at the River's mouth. On the shore of Lake Michigan there were several acres of pine sawdust, highly inflammable of course because of the drought. In addition, several hundred cords of dry pine slabs were piled along the River, to be used as fuel for tug boats.

When the firemen arrived, the hills circling the lake shore were already a ring of fire, which was beginning to roll down like a luminescent flood. The sawdust exploded into flame, creating a whirling windstorm. The burning dust was carried upwards into great clouds of fire which filled the air. The slabs of wood ignited, sending up sheets of flame that swayed like great banners. Columns of fire swept across the

Manistee River, which at that point was two hundred feet wide. The Government lighthouse, one hundred and fifty feet from the north bank of the River, burst almost instantly into flame.

Beside the mill on the lake shore were a large fleet of vessels tied up in the harbor. There were four tugs, three large barges and a huge steam tugboat called the Bismark. These were in great danger of burning. No one had ever seen a fire like it. It was more rapid and all-consuming than any normal fire.

Sailors, lumbermen and farmers fought together, working feverishly in the unearthly light, but they were no match for this fire. The engine broke down and it was no longer possible to play water on the flames. Everything was being swept away.

Then the men noticed a sudden bright light to the south of the town; a fierce wind suddenly sprang up, blowing toward Manistee. Some of the fire fighters decided to rush there in order to protect their homes and families. When they got there they found to their horror that the dead hemlock forest, twenty acres of brittle wood, south and east of the town was ablaze. For a few hours they managed to hold the fire. But after midnight the south wind became a tornado: fiery clouds containing sparks, cinders, burning bark and splinters hurled through the air. The fight was lost.

Each man fled to his house. Some of the hemlocks still stood seventy or eighty feet high, and the flames shot up to the tops of these, and then soared far beyond them in great curling tongues. One witness said later:

> The scene was grandly terrible beyond description. To us, whose homes and dear ones and all were in the track of the fire, it was heart-rending.
>
> Then came a deluge of fire, like that which rained on the [Biblical] cities of the plains. The wooden town, the sawdust streets, the stumpy vacant lots, the pine-clad hills north of the river, all burst into a sea of flames made furious by the most fearful gale of wind I have ever experienced.
>
> On toward the river and the Manistee Lake spread the tempest of fire. Men, women, and children, in night clothes, half clothed or fully clothed — some bareheaded, on foot, in wagons, on horseback — all fled for their lives. It was pandemonium.

A Detroit newspaper later carried the story of Allison Weaver, a foreman of a shingle mill near Port Huron, about two hundred miles from Manistee. Weaver, a fifty-year-old bachelor and a veteran of the Civil War, decided to remain with the mill when its owner and all the other employees fled before the fire that they knew was coming toward them. He had no property to lose, and no family to take care of: he said he decided to "stay and see the circus out." He was a stubborn man, and was more than ever determined to stay when the mill owner, a man named Bright, warned everyone to leave because he knew the fire was coming that way.

As soon as everyone left Weaver to work and buried all the provisions left behind, along with the knives, belts and other light machinery of the mill, as well as a stove and a lot of crockery. There was plenty of water in the vicinity of the mill: he filled several barrels full, and wet down the house, the mill, the stock and everything else he could think of that was inflammable, scattering several hundred pailsful of water on the ground around the buildings.

Night fell, and the fire which had been expected momentarily did not come. He thought to himself that his colleagues and his boss were a little too quick on the trigger. But about ten o'clock it grew so light that he could see each blade of grass, and a roaring commenced in the forest, sounding like waves beating against rocks on the shore.

He knew then that he was in for it, and he began to prepare further, more feverishly this time. When the ground had been leveled around the shingle mill, it had been necessary to dig up earth, leaving pits. Weaver dug one of these pits deep enough for him to stand in. Then he filled it with water, taking care also to saturate the ground around it for a good distance. He went to the mill, dragged out a four-inch plank, sawed it in two and fit the parts tightly over the mouth of what was now a small well. "I kalkerated it would be tech and go," he said, "but it was the best I could do."

By midnight, he felt he was ready, and the roaring in the woods was awful to hear. The clearing in which the buildings sat was about ten to twelve acres; Weaver said later that for about two hours before the fire reached him small animals fled constantly across the land. While he was resting for a moment after wetting down the house once more, he saw a horse dash into the clearing at full gallop, aiming straight for him. The animal was trembling with terror and excitement; it was a pitiable sight. Suddenly the horse gave a loud snort, veered off to run two or three times around the house, and then shot off into the woods like a rocket.

It was not long after this that the fire arrived. Weaver stood by his well, ready for the emergency, but at the same time curious to see the first flames. The roaring grew even louder, the air became oppressively heavy and clouds of dust and cinders showered down upon the clearing. Now he could see the flames through the trees. They did not run along the ground, or run from tree to tree, but they came on like a tornado: a sheet of flame reached from the earth to the top of the trees. As the sheet struck the clearing, he leaped into his well and pulled the planks over his head.

Now he could not see, but he could still hear. The flames went on roaring. He had hardly closed the opening over his head before the house and the mill were aflame. He said both burned down in about five minutes. The smoke came into his hiding place which grew so hot that he could hardly breathe.

The planks above him were on fire. He knew

that, but he counted on their thickness to protect him. When the roaring died away he pushed them over and dashed water from his hole with his hands over the wood to extinguish the burning. It was a cold night and he had at first been chilly standing in the water but gradually it became comfortably warm. He stayed in his den until daylight, frequently turning over the planks and dashing water on them to extinguish the fire.

When he suspected that the worst had passed, at dawn or a little later, he ventured out. The earth around the clearing was still burning in spots. The house and the mill were gone; so were leaves, brush and logs — all swept clean away as if they had been shaved off and then swept with a broom. Nothing but soot and ashes remained.

When things cooled down considerably, he dug up his buried treasure and found that a considerable amount of the buried property was intact. He lost all his provisions except a piece of dried beef, which the fire had cooked as though it were in an oven; it was not spoiled. He had to stay where he was all day, that night and a great part of the next day. By that time the ground had cooled enough so that he could pick his way to the site of the burned village.

It took him twelve hours to travel twelve miles because trees were falling, logs were still burning and the fallen timber in some places had become heaped up like a breastworks. He could not climb over it.

Miraculously there was not much loss of life in

Michigan, but ten to twenty thousand people there lost their homes and everything they owned.

The Michigan fire was on the east side of the Lake. At the same moment, on the west side, in and around Peshtigo, for miles, fireballs fell on housetops, and on streets. Men, women, children, horses, oxen, dogs, farm animals — all living things were seized by panic. A spectator commented that although much was said later of the intense heat of these fires, nothing that was said could really give even a faint conception of the reality. The heat had been compared to a flame concentrated by a blow-pipe, but even that would not account for some of the phenomena.

For instance [the spectator wrote] we have in our possession a copper cent, taken from the pocket of a dead man in the Peshtigo Sugar Bush... this cent has been partially fused but still retains its round form and the inscription upon it is legible. Others in the same pocket were partially melted off, and yet *the clothing and the body of the man was not even singed.* We do not know any way to account for this unless, as is asserted by some, the tornado and fire were accompanied by electrical phenomema.

The prevailing idea among the people was that the last day of the world had come. They were used to fires, but they had seen nothing like this in their lives. Their only interpretation of the terrifying roaring, the bursting of the sky with flame and the dropping down of fire from the heavens, consuming everything it touched, was that the Last Trump had sounded and the Day of Judgment was upon them.

No two people gave an exactly similar description of the great tornado as it struck and devoured the village. One said that it seemed as though "the fiery fiends of hell had been loosened." Another remarked, "It came in great sheeted flames from heaven." People spoke of "a pitiless rain of fire and sand," of the atmosphere "all afire," of "great balls of fire unrolling and shooting forth in streams." The fire leaped over roofs and trees and ignited whole streets at once. No one could stand before the blast. It was a race with death, above, behind and before them.

People ran for safety to the houses on the south side of the Peshtigo River and, across the narrow bridge, to the north side, where the lumber company, boarding house, warehouse and shops were. The boarding house, which was large, filled with anxious citizens, as did the company stores. The fire seemed confined to that part of the town which lay south of the river, so the north side seemed to offer shelter.

Among the refugees was a civil engineer who had registered for the night at the Peshtigo Hotel. He had reached the bridge over the river, but just as he was about to cross it, a mill on the north side burst inexplicably into flame. He hesitated, and the full horror of the situation burst upon him for the first time. There was fire on all sides of him; the bridge he was standing on was beginning to burn; the air was hot and filled with fire; cattle were bellowing, horses were running wild through the screaming crowds of panic-stricken people, and the wind was blowing a hurricane. A factory which manufactured wooden ware blew up before any fire could reach it.

He struggled back to the south side of the bridge with difficulty. Stampeding cattle knocked him down. But he got across and threw himself into the water. He made his way upstream, wading and sometimes swimming. He wanted to get as far from the burning buildings as possible. But the heat was increasing so rapidly that when he was about four hundred feet from the bridge and the nearest building, he had to lie down behind a log that was aground in about two feet of water. He managed to breathe by going under water only now and then, and by holding his head close to the water behind the log.

There were a dozen other people seeking shelter there. He knew that if he had actually been able to cross the river and enter the buildings on the other side, he would have been killed, as many people were. The river was four or five hundred feet wide at that point, and no one thought that the fire could cross it. But cross it it did.

Along with the demonic howling of the wind came a storm of fire. Eyewitnesses compared it to a snowstorm, but each snowflake was a burning coal. Flames were raining from the sky. Instantly nearly every building in the town north of the river, along with those on the south side which had remained miraculously untouched up to then, went up in flames. Houses crumbled as though they were made of paper. Their flaming roofs and entire walls were carried on the wind and ignited structures that had not as yet caught fire.

The wind was so powerful that no one could stand against it; they had to throw themselves to the ground in order not to be carried away themselves. Many of these people died from the fire; many who threw themselves into the river were drowned. Others who raised their heads from the water in order to breathe, drew flames into their lungs and died from that.

Accompanying the firestorm and the wind was a rain of red hot sand. It was not clear to those eyewitnesses who survived their ordeal where this sand came from. It must have been raised from the earth by the incredible winds, but from where? There was sand on the beaches, but the beaches lay to the east, and the wind was blowing from the west and the south. There was no sand on the floor of the forest nor on the farmlands of Wisconsin.

It is possible that this sand came from a comet, whose body, as we know, is made up partly of sand.

As inexplicable as the red hot sand are the stories of balloons of fire which many people told. There were for instance the Lawrences. Their farm, on the route south from Peshtigo to Green Bay, was one of the most prosperous in the area. It, like the town of Peshtigo, was overwhelmed with flames on that awful Sunday. The onslaught was so sudden that the family could only run to the center of an immense clearing on their farm where nothing combustible stood. They hoped to be safe, several hundred yards from structures or trees.

When the fire came, rushing on all sides of them, it did not in fact touch them. But eyewitnesses saw them die. A great balloon of fire dropped on them — father, mother and four children. They were incinerated in an instant. Almost nothing was left of them.

Many survivors described these great balls of fire falling from the sky. The whole sky was filled with them: round smoky masses about the size of a large balloon, traveling at unbelievable speed. They fell to the ground and burst. A brilliant blaze of fire erupted from them, instantly consuming everything it touched. It was hotter obviously than normal fire.

It is possible that these fireballs were actually flaming masses of methane and acetylene gas from a comet, ignited by their passage through the atmosphere. Witnesses had never seen anything remotely like them. No one who later read about this tragedy had ever experienced anything like them.

Another eyewitness was James B. Clark of Detroit, who was staying at Uniontown, Wisconsin, that Sunday night. He saw fires blazing through the forests and along the prairies in every direction. There was a strong breeze at sundown. At nine o'clock that night it increased to a furious gale, blowing toward the Lake. The whole surface of the country — westward, eastward, southward — seemed to be one mass of flame which almost reached to the clouds, which were somewhat low. The flame rushed along at race-horse speed. Beyond, toward the Lake, was the settlement of Williamson's Mills, where fourteen families lived.

The fire suddenly made a rush, Clark said, "like the flash of a train of gunpowder, and swept in the shape of a crescent around the settlement." It was almost impossible, he said, to conceive of the frightful rapidity of the flames. They seemed to eat up trees, to annihilate them. The roar of the blast was like the whirring of a giant mill. As he and others stood looking on, about ten o'clock they heard another strange sound. The fire was about seven miles from them, and they strained their eyes toward it: they could just make out something moving. Sometimes it looked like a black mass, then it seemed to separate into fragments, swaying to and fro, bobbing up and down. Whatever it was, it was coming toward them directly from a lurid wall of flame.

The light around them was so intense that their eyes were dazed; they kept blurring and they could only see if they kept wiping them with their handkerchiefs. Finally they made out, by sight as well as sound, that the moving mass was a stampede of cattle and horses, thundering toward them away from the flames, galloping with bellows and neighs. They finally came rushing past at incredible speed. Their eyeballs were distended with terror. They were delirious with fright. Some of them were already badly burned; they must have plunged desperately through walls of fire in order to escape.

Following behind them was a solitary horse, panting and snorting, nearly exhausted. He was saddled and bridled, and at first Clark thought he had a bag lashed to his back. But as he came closer it became apparent that a man lay fallen over the horse's neck, the bridle wound around his hands, and the mane clutched in his fingers. The horse was stopped — he was almost dead from exhaustion anyway, and the rider, who was little more than a boy, was taken into the house. He had inhaled the smoke and was at the point of death. He told them his name. It was Patrick Byrnes, and he said that his parents and the other children had gotten into a wagon and he did not know what had become of them.

Clark and his friends were spared, and the next morning he and some others drove down to the settlement, leaving Patrick Byrnes behind in critical condition. The first house they came to was Byrnes'. It was a heap of ashes. Only the brick chimney, the cooking stove and some iron farm tools remained. The forest had burnt down to the ground: only smouldering stumps remained. Everything was hot. Even the road was baked and cracked by the heat. About a mile farther on, they saw the bodies of six people and two horses, lying in a gully by the side of the road, roasted to a crisp. The iron tires of the wheels and the braces and bolts of the wagon were scattered about. The fire had surrounded and engulfed them, and the animals, in agony, had plunged and fallen off the road.

Understandably upset, Clark and his party hurried on. All along the road they found carcasses of animals: sheep, cattle, dogs, hogs — all burned to a crisp. In some cases the smaller animals were only piles of ashes.

When they came to the village, they found nothing but smoking, smouldering piles of ashes. In the cellar of one house were eight bodies. One man was still in a stooping position over what had evidently been a child. Undoubtedly he had been trying to ward off the flames. They assumed that this was Mr. Williamson, the owner of the mills, who had perished with his entire family. In the next yard were four bodies — a mother and her children. They were scorched but not burnt. Evidently they had suffocated. The most horrible thing they saw was Boorman's well. Boorman's was the largest house in the village; he supplied several of his neighbors with water from his well. Apparently these wretched people had leapt into this well as their last refuge. The chain and wheel pump had been removed. They had thrown boards down to prevent themselves from drowning, but so many of them had jumped into the well that some had drowned, some had been burnt and some had suffocated. In all, thirty-two bodies were found in that well, in every imaginable position, with contorted limbs and agonized expressions.

All the survivors said that the fire did not come gradually, from burning trees or houses,

borne by the wind, but that it came in a whirlwind of flame from above the tops of the trees.
Often the air itself, as we have noted before,
heated beyond endurance, was lethal to breathe.

12

Chicago, Late Sunday Night

After two o'clock in the morning, Joseph Edgar Chamberlain crossed the River, in a desperate attempt to reach his office on Madison Street beyond Clark. He pushed through the crowd on Randolph Street as far west as LaSalle Street where the Courthouse was burning. The cupola was ablaze as he came upon it; he found it a sight of sublime but melancholy beauty. After a while the great tower, undermined by the fire below it, fell to the bottom of the building with a dull thud and a heavy shock that shook the earth. Somebody called out "Explosion!" and the crowd, jarred into panic, began to run westward, carrying everyone with it.

Chamberlain worked himself free and went to Lake Street. A torrent of sparks was sweeping toward him down the street: he pulled his hat over his eyes, buttoned up his collar and rushed on eastward, still determined to reach his office. When he turned down Dearborn Street, he was greeted with a maelstrom of burning sparks which drove him into an open store, deserted by

Palmer House, Corner of State and Quincy Streets.

its occupants. They had left a large blanket lying on the floor. He wrapped it around his head and his body and went out again, getting as far as Washington Street. At this point he realized that to attempt to go any farther would be madness. He ran back to Lake Street and came down LaSalle again, where the fire was raging.

Wagons were rushing through the street loaded with goods, books, papers, boxes of everything conceivable; scores of frantic men were dragging trunks along the sidewalks, knocking down women and children. People were offering vast sums of money to truckmen if they would let them on their conveyances. It was an indescribable scene. Nevertheless, despite the people who were flying about in a panic, spectators stood silent in the street. They stood transfixed, staring at the fire, oblivious to the scurrying masses, torn with horror and admiration, and occasionally exclaiming involuntarily at the beauty of the scene.

The noise was terrific. In addition to the normal roar of any large fire, there was the crash of falling buildings and the constant explosions of stores of oil and other combustible materials. The noise of the crowd was puny compared to this. Chamberlain was overwhelmed: "All these things," he said, "the great, dazzling, mounting light, and the crash and roar of the conflagration, and the desperate flight of the crowd — combined to make a scene of which no intelligent idea can be conveyed in words."

When it became too hot for him to remain in

Randolph Street, he walked to the eastern approach of the bridge there. It was almost four o'clock in the morning by then. A knot of men stood near the bridge, silent and exhausted. The excitement of the night had worn away. Chamberlain, worn-out after two nights of intense activity, sank down on the railing and looked on what he later called the most appalling spectacle of the whole night:

> The Briggs House, the Metropolitan House, Peter Schuttler's wagon manufactory, Heath & Milligan's oil establishment stored five stories high with exceedingly inflammable material, the Nevada Hotel, and all the surrounding buildings were in a simultaneous blaze. The flames, propelled by variable gusts of wind, seemed to pour down Randolph Street in a liquid torrent. Then the appearance was changed, and the fire was a mountain over our heads. The barrels of oil in Heath's store exploded with a sound like rattling musketry. The great north wall of the Nevada Hotel plunged inward with hardly a sound, so great was the din of the surrounding conflagration. The Garden City House burned like a box of matches; the rapidity of its disappearance was remarked by everybody. Toward the east and the northeast we looked upon a surging ocean of flame.

Meanwhile a torrent of humanity was pouring over the bridge. The Madison Street bridge had long before become impassable, and Randolph was the only outlet for the entire region south of it. There were drays, express wagons, trucks — every kind of conveyance of every size — all crowded together and all hurrying across. Every moment there were collisions; and when one overloaded wagon broke down, there were enough men on hand to drag it and its contents over the bridge by force of hand.

The same long line of men dragging trunks that he had seen before, seemed to be there again. Many of them were struggling with loads that a horse would strain at. Women, as they had been all night, were staggering under the weights on their backs. There were whole brothels with their half-dozen employees loaded into the bottom of express wagons driven by their "men." Now and then a stray schooner which, because it had no tugboat, had been unable to escape sooner from the south branch, came up and demanded that the bridge be opened for it.

The people howled with rage; they could be heard above the other noises of the night. Above, in the stream, was a brig. The captain stood on the quarter-deck calling frantically to every passing tug. The crowd shouted to him to leave at once or he would lose his boat.

An undertaker rushed across the bridge; he headed a weird procession. He was holding a large coffin and he had given half a dozen boys a coffin each to carry:

> The sight of those coffins, upright, and bobbing along just above the heads of the crowd, without any apparent help from anybody else, was somewhat startling, and the unavoidable suggestion was that they were escaping across

Tribune Building.

Unity (Mr. Collyer's) and New England Churches.

the river to be ready for use when the debris of the conflagration would be cleared away. But just as men in the midst of a devastating plague carouse over each new corpse, and drink to the next one who dies, so we laughed quite merrily at the ominous spectacle.

Finally it became too warm for comfort on the east side of the River. The fire was burning along Market Street and people began to debate whether Lind's Block would go: the buildings opposite were burning with a furnace heat, but Lind's Block stood there, like a monument.

Then people began to discuss whether the City could recover from this desolation. The general consensus was that it could not. All capital had been wiped out; the next day there would not be an insurance company left. St. Louis would take the City's trade, or Cincinnati, or New York. There was nowhere left to transact business anyhow, even if there was to be any business, which there was not. The bombastic, energetic optimism that was a hallmark of Chicago had drained away from these men, who stood facing the burning city, watching great hotels and warehouses toppling, one after another, to the ground. The tension was terrible; they were ready to break.

Chamberlain joined the crowd moving up Canal Street, and lay down on a pile of lumber on the dock, where the North and South branches of the River met. He no longer cared about anything. His sensibilities were dead. There were half a dozen strangers lying there with him, and they were as listless as he was. All they talked about was how much one of their number weighed: he was a fat fellow named Fred. Chamberlain became interested and joined in the guessing. Finally Fred told them in confidence that he weighed two hundred and six pounds.

While this was going on, the Wells Street bridge took fire, distracting them once more. First the south end of the bridge lighted up, and then the north end, which burned more slowly. The whole structure tipped to the north and stood with one end in the water, at a sixty degree angle. Eventually, as the fire ate at it, it began to look like a skeleton with fiery ribs. When its supports were burned away, the skeleton turned a complete somersault and plunged into the River as if it were seeking refuge.

Meanwhile Alexander Frear, who had begun the evening at the Sherman House, returned there later in search of the children he referred to as "Mrs. Frear's children," who had unaccountably vanished. The Sherman House had already caught fire twice, and when Mr. Frear got there some men were on the roof smothering cinders, and a hose was playing on the building. The corridors by now were scenes of mass confusion. Guests ran about, some of them dragging their trunks to the stairway. Frear's heart sank as he saw that panic had spread among them. He glanced out of a window and was impressed with the "terribly magnificent" sight he saw there: the Courthouse Park was crowded with people, huddled togther in a solid mass, "helpless and astounded." The air was entirely filled with falling cinders, like a snowstorm lit by colored fire. The effect of the light upon the silent mass of people was frightful and unforgettable.

Frear's nephew turned up again, saying he had a horse and all he needed was a rubber blanket for it; he suggested Frear accompany him to see the fire. Frear mentioned Mrs. Frear and her despair over the missing children, but his nephew brushed this aside as relatively unimportant, and they set out in a light wagon for Wabash Avenue, stopping only briefly for coffee. Several firemen were in the coffeehouse — one bathing his head with whisky from a flask — and they said they were overworked, and the entire department was giving up; they could do nothing more. Someone brought in an Irish girl whose dress had almost been burnt off. A cinder had ignited it on the Courthouse steps.

Frear and his nephew left the café, to find a man in shirt-sleeves attempting to unhitch their horse. When they came up, he leapt into the wagon and would have driven off if Frear had not caught the horse's head. The man, beside himself, sprang out of the wagon, struck Frear's nephew in the face and ran off toward State Street.

Despite this ominous occurrence, Frear and his nephew drove rapidly into Wabash Avenue. The wind swept the cinders before them in furious waves. They passed a broken-down fire engine in the middle of the road. The storm of falling fire was growing worse; they could barely protect themselves from the burning rain and guide the horse at the same time through the frightened mob and the crush of vehicles. Frear looked back toward the Opera House, in the direction they had come, and saw smoke and flames pouring out of State Street. The area they had just left was on fire, and the intervening space was filled with whirling embers that beat against the houses, and covered the roofs and windowsills. It was a tornado of fire. Wabash Avenue was burning as far down as Adams Street. Animals, burnt and terrified by the cinders, darted through the streets, ignoring all humans who got in their way. The flames from the houses on the west side reached in a diagonal arch across the street and occasionally the wind lifted the great body of flames, detached it entirely from the burning buildings and hurled it far ahead with terrific force.

No one was making any attempt to put out fires. The mansions on Wabash Avenue were being emptied amidst tremendous confusion and disorder. A mob of men and women, all screaming and shouting, ran about wildly, getting in each others' way, bumping into one another as if they had lost their minds. The Avenue was littered with expensive furniture , some of it ignited by the falling sparks. Twice Frear and his nephew were accosted by gentlemen who held out pocket books and requested that they carry an item of value away to safety. Women came and threw packages into the wagon; one man with a boy clinging around his neck caught the horse and tried to push the two men out. Finally Frear alighted and tried to lead the horse out of the street.

They had not gone a block before they noticed that the Courthouse was on fire; at the same moment they heard that the St. James Hotel roof had caught. A bird-cage, flung from an upper window, hit Frear's arm; startled, he released the horse, which shied and ran into a burning dray filled with furniture; the wheel of the wagon was smashed and the nephew was thrown out onto his shoulder, which was badly bruised. The horse had had enough: he disappeared down the street with "a leap like that of a panther."

The two men hurried toward the St. James Hotel. They saw a woman kneeling in the street holding a crucifix up before her; the skirt of her dress was on fire. A runaway truck smashed into her as she prayed. Repeatedly trucks passed with their loads of goods burning; Frear's nephew later swore that he saw a man go up to a pile of costly furniture that was lying in front of an impressive mansion and deliberately hold a piece of burning packing board under it until it ignited.

When they reached the wholesale district north of Madison Street things were, if possible, even worse. There were no police and no firemen, no one to protect merchandise that was doomed anyway because of the wild advance of the fire. A few of the porters and drivers employed by these firms were attempting to protect the stores, but a huge crowd of men and boys were tearing open parcels to see what was in them, and throwing all sorts of property onto a motley assortment of wagons, carts and even coaches.

Between one and two in the morning, Frear reached the St. James Hotel where women and children were screaming and running about in every direction and baggage was being thrown about recklessly. Hundreds of people, he heard, had vanished in the flames. Mrs. Frear, he learned, had been taken unconscious to the home of a friend on the North side. He feared her children were lost. People came into the hotel saying that the Sherman House was going, and that the Opera House had caught. Finally the word was that the bridges were on fire, and that all escape was cut off to the North and West.

This caused an indescribable scene: the news was shouted loudly by men and women, many of whom, half-dressed and with screaming children, fled the building. A jam occurred in the doorway, where people struck and clawed at each other in an effort to get free. Frear's nephew was separated from him and he could not find him. Frear got out with the crowd and ran toward the Tremont House. On Dearborn Street the gust of wind was so strong that it almost knocked him off his feet.

At the Tremont House the situation was even worse than at the St. James. The elevator was jammed, and women were screaming for help from the upper floors. He saw no fire, so he forced his way upstairs, and looked into all the open rooms, calling out the names of Mrs. Frear's daughters. The parlors were swarming with women; invalids lay on the floor. Men stood, pale and silent, watching distracted women calling for their husbands.

During all this, the upper part of the Tremont House caught fire. Frear looked out of a window and saw the street below choked with screaming, moaning people. Far up Dearborn Street he could see the huge flames pouring in from the side streets that he had traveled through only an hour before; it appeared to him that they were impelled with the force of a tremendous blow-pipe. Everything that they touched melted.

Presently the smoke began to roll down the stairways; almost immediately the men who had been trying to smother the flames on the roof came running down. They rushed out of the building, without speaking, as though their lives depended on it. Frear, undaunted, went up to the fourth floor and looked in every room, kicking open those doors that were locked. He did not speak to several other men who were doing the same thing. From the fourth floor he had an excellent view: the fire was advancing steadily upon the hotel from two or three points. There was little smoke; the fire was burning too rapidly, and the wind was too strong. A loud crackling noise accompanied the flames, like an enormous bundle of dry twigs burning, and there were constant explosions in rapid succession coming from all sides.

On the stairs, he came upon a man dragging

an unconscious woman down by her shoulders. She was unusually large and wore a striped satin dress and a good deal of jewelry, no doubt worn to be saved from destruction. Frear helped carry her and when they reached the bottom of the staircase she recovered consciousness suddenly, much to Frear's surprise, and moved off quickly, followed by the man.

All down Dearborn Street people swayed and surged under the rain of fire. On Lake Street a man loaded a truck with silks from Shay's dry goods store, ignoring the threats of the employees. One man threatened to shoot him if he attempted to drive away. "Fire," the thief cried, "and be damned!" The employee pocketed his pistol and the man drove away. East of Shay's store at least a ton of fancy goods had been thrown into the street. People walked and drove over them; eventually they caught fire.

On the Clark Street bridge lay a ragged boy who had been killed by a marble slab which had evidently been thrown from a window. He was wearing white kid gloves and his pockets were stuffed with gold-plated sleeve-buttons. An Irish woman walked across the bridge, leading a pregnant goat; she carried a piece of silk under her arm. On Lake Street the stores were filled with thieves who were flinging out merchandise to accomplices in the street where fights were starting over possession of it.

Wabash Avenue was glutted with people and abandoned possessions. People had come there from all over the city and, being stopped by the

River, had dropped everything in their panic. Valuable oil paintings were trampled underfoot, along with books, pet animals, musical instruments, toys, mirrors and bedding. Goods from the stores had been dragged out and caught fire; the crowd had broken into a liquor store and were brandishing champagne and brandy bottles and yelling at the tops of their lungs. It was a brutal and horrible scene.

A man stood on top of a piano and announced that the fire was the poor man's friend. He urged everyone to help themselves to all the best liquor they could get. He continued to shout from the piano until someone threw a bottle at him and knocked him off.

Through the chaos wandered hundreds of children, crying for their parents. One little girl ran past whose golden hair, loose down her back, caught fire. Someone threw a glass of liquor on her; it flared up and covered her with a blue flame.

By this time dawn had broken. The fire raged around Frear, who fought his way back to Randolph Street. The Courthouse, the Sherman House, the Tremont House, the wholesale stores on Wabash Avenue and the retail stores on Lake Street were all burning. The cries of the people on the streets there had risen to a terrible roar: the flames were breaking now into the streets bordering the River. The stores ignited suddenly all over, just as paper does when it is held to the fire. The crowds greeted each outburst of flame with hoarse shouts.

In one of the stores a number of men were on the several floors passing out goods; when the flames blew over and enveloped the building, they were lost to sight. Nobody made any attempt to save them because the heat was so intense that it was like a tornado, driving everyone back. Frear was carried by the momentum of the crowd back to Lake Street. He struggled to get to the River and did so, almost at the cost of his life. The bridge railing had broken away and a good many people were pushed into the water. One man, loaded with clothing, stumbled and fell; he disappeared. A number of small boats carrying goods were passing up and down the River; their occupants did not pay the slightest attention to the unfortunates who tumbled into the water around them, or to the people on the bridge, except to make sure that no one fell into their boats.

Once over the River, Frear felt safe. The River was widest at that point and he was positive that the fire could not leap over it. He walked through North Water Street, running into frantic mobs from each of the bridges. It took him a long time to get to the West Side, and his sister's house. When he got there, his nephew had arrived before him, and told him that Mrs. Frear was safe in a private house on Huron Street.

Frear was wet, scorched and bedraggled. On his arms, shoulders and back, his clothes were burnt full of holes. He asked his nephew to make him some coffee, and he fell down in the hallway and went to sleep. About half an hour later his nephew woke him, saying that the fire was sweeping through Lincoln Park, and that Mrs. Frear was probably not safe after all. They both went out again, and ran as fast as they could go toward the North Side. By this time it was eight-thirty in the morning.

They could see across the River at the cross streets that the City was now a mass of smoking ruins. Thousands of people wandered around; but their excitement had given way to terrible feelings of grief and desolation. Mrs. Frear was retrieved from the house on Huron Street; they found a baker's wagon to put her in; she was completely hysterical. An omnibus filled with frightened children passed them. Mrs. Frear heard the children crying and screaming and began to scream loudly herself. The man who was driving the omnibus stopped and demanded to know where they were taking that woman; he thought she was being abducted.

Finally they reached their home. A number of neighbors came in to help calm Mrs. Frear. It was four o'clock in the afternoon before word came that the children were safe in Riverside. Frear spent a good part of the day looking for her property, to no avail, but by afternoon he was forced to go to bed with a sick headache and a fever, which he believed were caused entirely by psychological rather than physical factors.

Horace White, then editor of the *Tribune*, lived at Michigan Avenue, between Monroe and Adams Streets. He did not think the fire would last the night and went to the *Tribune* office to write about it. While there, he saw the flames breaking out of the roof of the Courthouse: since he knew that the fire had to leap a vacant space of nearly two hundred feet to get at the Courthouse roof, he surmised that most of the business section of the City was endangered. But it did not occur to him that the City Water Works, with their four great pumping engines, were in a straight line with the fire and the wind, and he did not know then that this machinery was housed in a building with a wooden roof.

He saw the tall buildings on opposite sides of the two streets melt down in a few moments. The heat broke the plate-glass windows in the lower stories of the Tribune Building. The upper story windows were untouched, and the composing and editorial roooms did not even smell of smoke. Supposing that the danger was now past, White went home to breakfast. The smoke in the North Division was so dense that nothing could be seen there, although sixty thousand people were fleeing before the flames. The Field store was being showered with water by Field's own fire engines and the First National Bank building on the corner was fireproof, so White assumed that that area at least was protected. Fireproof buildings like the Bank, the Tribune, the Post Office and the Customs House would stop the flames, he thought.

Nevertheless he and his family decided to remove their valuables from the house. White took a bird-cage containing a talented parrot and climbed up on a seat next to the driver of one of his wagons which contained a good deal of household treasure. They made fair progress south from the corner of Monroe Street. The dust was so thick they could not see ahead.

The obstruction came from a steady stream of sand, which drove against their faces like needle points. They reached the Park, but when they came to an excavation recently dug by the City, they had to return to Michigan Avenue. Millionaires were dragging trunks and bundles out of their mansions, but White said he saw no panic and no frenzy. He finally left his wagon at the home of a friend on Wabash Avenue, on the windward side of the fire, and went back to get another load.

He met his family half-way down Michigan Avenue, their arms filled with possessions. Mrs. White told him that their house was burned; the entire family was covered with dirt and soot.

The Tribune Building, despite its fireproof construction, was doomed, along with the Palmer House and all the buildings in the theatre district. William Bross, a publisher of the *Tribune*, commented that "Every bank and insurance office, law offices, hotels, theatres, railroad depots, most of the churches and many of the principal residences of the city" were a charred mass. Joseph Medill, seeing the Tribune Building was doomed, had found and purchased a job printing-office at Canal Street, so that the newspaper could be brought out.

Lambert Tree was among those people who sought refuge along the Lake front. When he and his family arrived — the women already hatless and slightly burned — they found thousands of men, women and children and hundreds of horses and dogs already there. The ground was covered with piles of trunks, chairs, tables, beds and other household furniture of every kind.

They stood at the Lake front between three and four o'clock in the morning and watched the fire gradually advance and encircle them: the whole city in every direction was a mass of smoke and flames. Whole families huddled around the little piles of furniture which were all that was left of their worldly goods. Here and there a mother sat on the ground holding a baby or small children who were asleep, exhausted by their experience. Relatives and friends clustered around invalids who lay on mattresses, frightened and worn out. Tree saw a young girl sitting near him with a cage containing a canary. She had the cage in her lap; it was covered by a shawl, and from time to time she peeked under the covering to make sure that the bird was all right. After an hour or so, she got up to move to another spot, and the little bird tumbled off his perch to the bottom of the cage. It was dead. The girl dissolved into inconsolable tears.

Some men and women had found liquor among the piles of household stores, and were reeling about, drunk. Several evil-looking men were breaking open trunks and boxes and rifling them. There were judges and police officers among the crowd but their authority was meaningless in that setting. A woman who had been brought in extremely ill, and who lay on the ground on a mattress, died in the midst of the crowd. Everyone knew that she had died, but the general reaction was one of comparative indifference.

Sparks and cinders were falling as fast as hailstones in a storm and soon after daybreak the piles of household goods which covered the ground began to burn. Feather beds and hair mattresses gave off so much heat and smoke that people were forced to work their way closer to the water. An hour later the immense piles of lumber to the south caught fire and it became difficult to breathe in the ensuing clouds of smoke and cinders. People, horses, dogs and all their vehicles had to enter the water. Some people drove their horses into the Lake as far as they could safely go; men, women and children sat on the wagons, and the Lake was lined with people standing in the water at various depths from their knees to their waists, with their backs turned to the firestorm behind them.

This went on for several hours until the lumber yards had virtually burnt themselves out. Tree moved slowly with his family to the north as far as the foot of Superior Street, where a wooden one-story building was still standing. They went inside, seeking relief from the polluted air which was causing their eyes to burn. But the building was crowded with people, and the air was, if possible, worse inside than it had been outside. The family settled down behind the north wall of Superior Street. Mrs. Tree was exhausted and sank down upon the ground. She had not been there very long before Tree noticed that her clothes were on fire. He beat out the fire with his hands, and the family decided that the safest thing for them to do was keep moving.

Between five and six o'clock in the afternoon a covered one-horse grocery wagon emerged from the smoke in Superior Street. Tree ran to stop it, and arranged with the driver to take as many people as possible to the West Side for ten dollars. Eleven people and a pet goat were squeezed into the wagon; little could be seen through the smoke, but enough was visible so that everyone knew that the North Side had been destroyed: all that was left there were a few chimney stacks and a broken wall here and there. The rest of the houses lay in the smouldering embers and tangled debris of the cellars.

When they reached the West Side, it was seven o'clock at night. They did not know where to tell the driver to take them. They had not eaten since five o'clock dinner on Sunday, twenty-six hours earlier. The driver stopped before a boarding-house, where Tree recognized Charles Gray, who lived in the area, and who invited him and his family to stay with him. They accepted grate-

Chamber of Commerce.

City Hall.

fully, but it was not a restful night. Everyone was terrified that a change of wind would bring the fire close to them again, and the water supply was entirely cut off. Citizens were patrolling the streets: smoking was prohibited there. Tree stayed up most of the night taking his turn at patrol.

At daybreak he hailed an express wagon and went to the North Side to look for a trunk of silver which he had buried. No house stood to the north, south or east of Wells Street except the Ogden House. The telegraph wires lay curled and tangled on the streets, along with dead horses, cows and other animals. Tree saw only one human corpse: it was on Dearborn between Ohio and Ontario and was burned beyond recognition.

Michael W. Conway, the pipeman of the steam [fire engine] "Chicago" testified at the hearing in November, 1871, that he worked on the Saturday night fire until four-thirty Sunday afternoon, when his eyes were full of cinders and he was physically and emotionally exhausted. He went home to sleep and his wife woke him about eleven o'clock Sunday night; she was afraid their house was in danger. He went over to the engine house, which was on Jefferson Street near Van Buren. Someone said the fire was on the South Side, but he did not believe it; he thought the reflection of the West Side fire created an illusion.

The fire engine was not working, and six hundred feet of hose that had been in the engine house on Sunday afternoon had been lost. There was no one around to give him any directions, but the foreman told Conway he could take the engine; he himself was too tired to do anything. Conway crossed the Randolph Street bridge and went east. He passed the Courthouse and noticed that the roof was on fire, but just as he was about to attach the suction to a fire plug, several men came out of the cupola with buckets and brooms and he decided that the Courthouse fire was a small one and the men could manage it. He worked on Franklin Street near Washington, and then on Randolph Street, where he played water on the buildings on the south side of the street.

The flames, he said, came from the basements of the stores, while there was no sign of fire in any other part of the building. Once he saw a woman looking out of a fourth floor window: he threw stones against the window to attract her attention and told her to get out of the building at once. Just as she reached the street, flames burst out of the basement windows. The fire seemed to be coming from the east down Randolph Street. Conway said that the light of the fires in the cellars was a strange light; it looked as if whisky or alcohol were burning. He heard explosions all through the night and assumed that they were caused by falling walls, because he knew of no one who was blowing anything up. A perfect gale was blowing, the air was oppressively warm and filled with sparks and his eyes were painful and streaming.

He saw the Metropolitan Hall burn, and he did not think it remained standing a minute after the fire started. The dome of the Briggs House caught fire. The only drunks he saw were civilians, he said; he saw no drunken firemen.

Fire Marshal Williams testified that he and his men had done the best they could: waves of flame kept pouring over his men and they could not work. When he went south and got to Monroe Street he found that the Gas Works was on fire and that the Armory and the block up to Wells Street was going fast. He played water on Monroe Street but he soon realized that the whole thing was hopeless; the fire was leaping over their heads and the gas reservoir could easily explode and blow everything up. So they left and went to Madison Street where there was a fire in the rear of the Oriental Building. They worked the engine on the corner of Washington and LaSalle Streets but they were not in the building for three minutes before a sheet of flame rolled over them and they dropped everything and ran for their lives.

"The wind was blowing so heavy at the time that the water would not go ten feet from the nozzle of the pipe," the Marshal said. "We could not strike a second story window. When we came through the stairway on LaSalle Street, the Court-house was on fire, and the next thing the Board of Trade was ablaze." It was suggested by an alderman that buildings be blown up, but the Marshal thought that the fire was going so fast they could not even make a start at that. He suggested the alderman empty the building on the southwest corner of LaSalle and Washington and blow it up. He himself then went to play water on the Sherman House to keep it from burning. He thought that was possible because it was surrounded by open space. "But my God!" the Marshal said, "there was a piece of board six feet long that came over and landed right on top of the Tribune Building on Clark Street and it was not two minutes before that row was on fire ... from there it went in all directions."

The fire then moved to the rear of the Sherman House and after that, Marshal Williams was overwhelmed by confusion. "I couldn't tell how it did go," he said. "It went whichever way it pleased."

It is significant that Pipeman Conway noticed flames coming from the *basements* of stores, while the upper floors of the buildings were not yet touched by fire. It is conceivable that cometary gases, which are heavier than air, had settled in these low spots and taken fire. When he signalled the woman on the fourth floor to leave the building, she no sooner did so than fire spurted from the basement windows of her building. And Conway commented specifically that the fire looked as though whisky or alcohol were burning. The chemical components of methane and acetylene, the cometary gases, are similar to the chemicals that form the basis of alcohol.

Burning of the Central Grain Elevator at the Mouth of the Chicago River.

The fire advanced more quickly than the firemen had ever seen fire advance before. It was everywhere: underfoot, overhead, all around them. It ran along dry roofs, sending blue smoke curling out from the eaves, and then bursting into a great mass of flame. Windows blew outwards in great explosions followed by torrents of fire. And the heat was incredible. Massive stone and brick structures literally melted before the astonished eyes of the on-lookers. Six-story buildings blazed up and disappeared forever in five minutes or less. In nearly every street flames began at the rear and then suddenly the fronts of the buildings erupted without warning.

The windows reddened suddenly and exploded with billows of fire. The only similar kind of fire was burning at this very moment hundreds of miles to the north. In Chicago the heat was so intense that blocks of Athenian marble burned along with dry wood. This fire, it would seem, must have been caused by exploding gases. These gases, having been carried ahead of the fire by the intense wind, would have penetrated and filled the buildings. When the sparks and burning debris landed on the buildings and the roofs and window-frames ignited, the gas would of course instantly burst into flame in all parts of the structure, and the flame would throw off immense heat, explosive heat.

Five hours after the first alarm was sounded, the flames leaped from the South to the North part of the City, across the River. An hour later the fire had become a single sheet of flame from

Rush to Clark Street, moving northeast. There was no hope of stopping it. Marshal Williams said that when he heard that the Water Works were on fire, and drove there to make sure that was true, he made up his mind then that the whole city was gone. "There was no possible chance for the North Side," he said, "any more than there was for the South."

There were great breweries near the Water Works at the Lake. By half-past three in the morning, less than two hours after the fire had spread to the North Division, the breweries were burning and the engineers and firemen in the Water Works building had had to flee because the shingle roof of the Water Works was on fire. The rafters fell in and disabled the machinery that was feeding water to the fire fighters. The water tower, miraculously, still stood, but the huge pumps had stopped.

The flames rolled eastward to the Lake, and had to stop there. But in the rest of the City, northward and southward, the sheets of flame kept moving. By ten on Monday morning the fire extended from the North branch of the River on the west to the Lake on the east, and was moving directly north as far as Fullerton Avenue.

Seventy-five thousand people were forced to flee for their lives. There was no island of safety except the waters of the Lake.

The First National Bank building was supposed to be fireproof. A row of marble-fronted brick buildings protected it on the south and on the west. It stood on a street that was one hundred feet wide. Nevertheless, once the window casings caught fire, sparks may have ignited the furniture. In any case the heat inside the building was so intense that the great iron girders that supported it expanded, the iron ceilings broke and fell, crashing against the exterior walls, and soon all that was left of the building was twisted metal and rubble.

The Tribune Building too was supposedly fireproof. It was believed that if all the furniture in the building were gathered into one room and ignited the building itself would not burn. However, the furniture did catch fire; the intense heat here too caused the iron girders and ceilings to expand and break out the walls, which, it had been said, would withstand any natural disaster. The Tribune Building also was reduced to rubble.

Hundreds of tons of pig iron bars were stacked in the yard of an agricultural implement factory on the River bank, and about two hundred feet from any building. When the factory caught fire, the incredible heat melted the iron bars and turned them to liquid. One large mass of metal was fused when the liquid cooled.

This was the story throughout the City that dreadful night. Coils of anchors and cables which were stored on the sidewalks in front of warehouses melted into solid masses when the warehouses burned.

The wind was generally considered to have been responsible for the fury and swiftness of the fire. William B. Ogden, the first mayor of

Chicago, wrote to a member of his family:

> The fire was accompanied by the fiercest tor-
> nado of wind ever known to blow here, and it
> acted like a perfect blow-pipe, driving the bril-
> liant blaze hundreds of feet with so perfect a
> combustion, that it consumed the smoke, and its
> heat was so great that fire proof buildings sunk
> before it, almost as readily as wood. Nothing but
> earth could withstand it.

The wind may well have raised the temperature
of the fire to a degree hot enough to ignite the
incendiary gases carried by a dying comet, and
deposited on three vulnerable areas at half-past
nine on that awful Sunday night in October, 1871.

13

Charred Wastes

On October 9, 1871, the Mayor of Chicago, R.B. Mason, issued a proclamation. In the Providence of God, he said, a terrible calamity had befallen the City, which demanded the best efforts of the citizens to preserve order and relieve suffering.

The headquarters of the City Government would be at the Congregational Church on the corner of West Washington and Ann Streets. The faith and credit of the City were pledged for the necessary expenses of relieving suffering and preserving order. The Police, and Special Police which were being appointed, were responsible for the maintenance of peace and the protection of property. All officers and men of the Fire Department and Health Department were appointed to act as Special Policemen without further notice. Vouchers would be given by the Mayor and the Comptroller for all supplies furnished by different Relief Committees. And all persons were warned that any acts which endangered property would be punished by immediate arrest:

With the help of God, order and peace and

private property shall be preserved. The City Government and committees of citizens pledge themselves to the community to protect them, and prepare the way for a restoration of public and private welfare.

It was believed, the Mayor added, that the fire had spent its force and all would soon be well.

On the same day, the Governor of Wisconsin, Lucius Fairchild, issued a proclamation from the Capitol at Madison to the people of Wisconsin:

Throughout the northern part of this State fires have been raging in the woods for many days, spreading desolation on every side. It is reported that hundreds of families have been rendered homeless by this devouring element, and reduced to utter destitution, their entire crops having been consumed. Their stock has been destroyed, and their farms are but a blackened desert. Unless they receive instant aid from portions not visited by this dreadful calamity, they must perish.

In Michigan the destruction was not so terrible as it was in Wisconsin; nevertheless between ten and fifteen thousand people were homeless.

In Wisconsin twelve hundred people had died in that single night. Four hundred farms had been destroyed, and those who survived were in deep shock. The least injured had burned faces and hands and feet. But some faces were burned raw, hands were black claws. Children were maimed, their feet severely burned. One widow had lost her crippled son, who was on crutches and could not outrun the flames. Her daughter

Where the Fire Began.

*Ogden's Residence. Only Residence Left
on North Division of Burned District.*

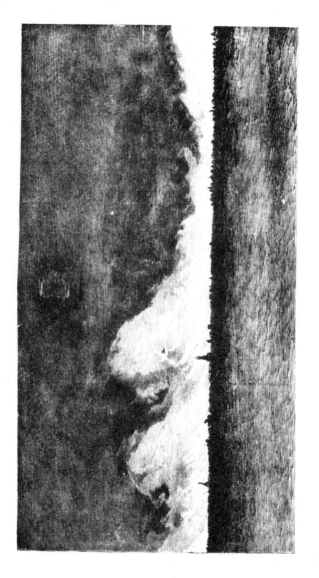

"The Great Conflagration," as Seen from the Prairie.

City Hall, After the Fire.

fell between the burning logs of their cabin. These two children were her whole family, and they were gone. She said over and over again that their screams were forever sounding in her ears.

A survivor wrote a letter to the Milwaukee *Wisconsin* telling about his travels through the ruined land. He rode several miles from Menominee to the opening in the woods where Peshtigo used to be. The road was level and sandy, bordered mainly by blackened stumps: the Fox River, where so many went for refuge, and where many died, was flowing placidly over the half-burnt dam. Heaps of mortar, brick and iron were all that remained of factories, mills, the foundry and the machine works. Everything else was covered by drifted ashes and sand.

He forded the river with his team and drove a few miles westward into the Sugar Bush settlements. Great forests of maple, oak, beech, hemlock and pine had been torn up by the tornado, and hurled crosswise and lengthwise on the ground. Not one tree in twenty was standing; the whole forest had been mowed down like grass.

The black wrath of the flames was also visible. Green maples and oaks, three feet in diameter, had gone down in a whirl and were eaten up by the flames in an hour. It was this double rage of tornado and flame, said the writer, that burst in upon the ill-fated village of Peshtigo. "Not all the fire steamers in the world could have stayed its destruction."

Though many more people had died in Wisconsin than in Chicago, the loss of property was far greater in Chicago. In the North Division, almost all the houses were destroyed: a black swath one mile wide and three miles long was cut through the heart of a busy community.

Everything that would burn was gone, including the sidewalks. And in the South Division destruction was no less, although most of the buildings there were built of stone and brick. Indeed, James W. Sheahan and George P. Upton, associate editors of the *Tribune*, commented that "the destruction of many of the heaviest stone buildings was much more rapid than that of wooden buildings, as they had become so thoroughly heated that the moment the flame seized upon them and swept through them, they melted away and disappeared." There had never been a parallel, they said, to the intensity and ferocity of that fire:

> It twisted iron into all manner of fanciful shapes. In crockery stores, it fused glass and china together in beautiful forms, and many sight-seers, after the ruins of such stores had cooled, carried away as relics great masses of glass, china, mortar, brick and earthen ware, cemented together in the most incongruous manner.

The blocks of pavement in some streets burned to the earth beneath. Rails of street railroads were twisted into perfect U's, which stood inverted.

> In such seething masses of flames, chasing after each other for twelve hours like billows along a beach, the very Pyramids would have yielded had they received the full force of the fire.

Michigan Southern R.R. Depot.

Palmer House, State Street.

Chamber of Commerce and Courthouse.

Post Office and Customs House.

In the South Division only two buildings still stood. One, at the corner of LaSalle and Monroe Streets, was a stone structure which had not been completed: the floors and partitions were brick, and no woodwork had yet been put in. Small wooden structures adjoined it, and those opposite it were also of stone, but they were only twenty feet deep and they collapsed almost at once. The Lind Block, the other building left intact, was comparatively isolated.

The Division, the editors said, was the heart of the city. Every newspaper office, both daily and weekly, every public library, every place of amusement, every bank except one, every first-class hotel with one or two exceptions, the two great depots, every insurance office, seven churches, every important public building, the Gas Works, the post office, the customs house, the marine hospital, several Roman Catholic charitable institutions, the City Hall, the Chamber of Commerce, every art gallery, the telegraph office, nearly every law and doctor's office, all the best restaurants, two commercial colleges, thousands of business offices, and all the great wholesale warehouses, piled with goods for the Autumn trade — all were totally ruined. "The wreck," they said, "was as complete as the wreck of Pompeii and Herculaneum."

Frederick Law Olmstead wrote a letter to the *Nation*, in which he too described the destruction. Everything smelled, he said, of charred earth. In not more than a dozen cases were the four walls of any buildings left standing. It was unusual to find even a single corner or chimney holding together to a height of more than twenty feet. One could see, from the top of a bus, for three miles across what had been the densest, most substantially built-up part of the City. Generally, he said, the walls seemed to have crumbled in from top to bottom; only a wide heap of rubbish remained, in the cellars, below the level of the pavement:

Granite, all sandstones and all limestones, whenever fully exposed to the southwest, are generally flaked and sealed, and blocks, sometimes two and three feet thick, are cracked through and through. Marble and other limestones, where especially exposed, as in doors and window dressings, especially if in thin slabs, have often fallen to powder. Walls of the bituminous limestone, of which there were but few, instead of melting away, as was reported, seem to have stood rather better than others, I cannot tell why. Iron railings and lamp-posts, detached from buildings, are often drooping and in thinner parts, seem sometimes to have fused. Iron columns and floor-beams are often bent in a half-circle.

Olmstead did not know why this happened. The drought, he thought, had something to do with it, but he could not put the blame on that alone. And as to the wind, he believed that many cities had droughts as bad as Chicago's drought was that Autumn, and experienced with it a wind as strong, without the accompanying conflagration. "The origin of the fire," he concluded somewhat weakly, "was probably a commonplace accident."

The fire started in a wooden building, and moved rapidly to others and the accumulated heat in the atmosphere gave rise to local currents whch drove burning heated brands onto the roofs and cornices of buildings to leeward and they caught fire... Their contents, piled tier on tier, burst into flame and generated an untoward degree of heat.

The month of October was a cataclysmic one for three regions around Lake Michigan. It surely could not have been a coincidence that fires, which had been burning normally, that is to say under control and offering no serious danger to life, should suddenly, at exactly the same time on the same night, hundreds of miles apart, burst out with an unprecedented fury and become impossible to control. Was it the continuous violent wind which, feeding the flames richly with oxygen, was responsible for temperatures so high that buildings melted before the horrified eyes of witnesses?

And how to explain the hot sand that rained down in the woods of Wisconsin? Were these particles scooped up by the tornado from some beach and then heated by the incandescent air before they fell — or is there another, more likely explanation for them?

And then there were the balloons of fire. Can these frightening phenomena be satisfactorily explained? What caused clouds of searing flame to fall from the sky on people, buildings, farmland and woods?

Fragments of a dead comet with its frozen

gases, its cargo of sandy cosmic debris, which intersect Earth's orbit and crash into its surface in the worst possible place at the worst possible time — in drought-stricken regions where fires are already burning... This would explain all the peculiar features of the great three-headed fire of October, 1871.

The wind where the Comet had landed was a gale. The gases in the Comet were freed from their frozen prison. Molecules of methane and acetylene, which require high temperatures to ignite — higher, that is, than the five hundred or so degrees at which wood ignites — reached that high temperature quickly because of the blowtorch effect of the wind feeding oxygen to the flames. The fires at the three places where the Comet had struck were fueled.

Sand grains from the Comet, which had been heated by its plunge through the atmosphere and by the fiery air into which they had fallen, rained on the earth. The tremendous heat of the fire ignited the clouds of gases which were trapped inside the Comet, the clouds exploded into flame and fire balloons were the result. When the cometary fuel was exhausted, the fires gradually burned themselves out.

This is one explanation for the incredible events of that Autumn night in the American Midwest. Death and destruction rained upon the Lake Michigan region and the cause of it remained anonymous. Because no one imagined that the earth was struck by a comet at 9:30 P.M. Central Standard time on Sunday night, October 8, 1871.

Charred Wastes

View from Harrison Street North on Wabash Avenue.

Masonic Temple, Dearborn Street.

14

Göttingen, Germany and Madras, India November, 1872

In 1852, 1859 and 1866 Biela's Comet could not be seen. Astronomers did not know what had become of it; their bewilderment found expression in the Annual Report of the Council of the Royal Astronomical Society in 1866. It was believed that the Comet, or Comets, was, or were, lost, and almost no one held any hope that it, or they, would reappear at the next estimated time of passage in 1872.

Since 1798 it had been noted that often in November there had been strong meteor showers: it was thought that the meteors had originated from a point in the constellation Andromeda, and therefore the meteor shower was called Andromedes. Astronomers began to notice that the showers became much brighter every six or seven years. The Italian astronomer Giovanni Schiaparelli traced the meteors through the path of a comet, and it was established that meteors were related to comets. Edmund Weiss, an Austrian astronomer, demonstrated through careful calculations that a meteor shower observable in late November of each year might be connected with Biela's Comet. He thought that there would be a major meteor shower in November, 1872, when the Earth passed through Biela's orbit.

This prediction turned out to be correct. There was a brilliant meteor shower on November 27, 1872. Weiss, who believed that Biela had broken up in the sixties, called the show "Bielids" rather than "Andromedes" because the shower had appeared when Biela itself should have appeared; he believed that the shower was the disintegrated remains of Biela, and many scientists today agree with him.

It had been determined that most, if not all meteor showers are essentially cometary debris, bits of sand, gravel, icy chunks of water and gases given off by the head of the comet during its swing around the Sun. The debris becomes the Comet's tail, but often lags behind it or moves ahead of it in its path. Eventually the debris spreads out along the full orbit of the Comet, providing, both behind and before it, a great ellipse of cometary fragments. Each time the Earth intersects the Comet's orbit bits of cometary residue come into our atmosphere and are consumed by friction.

However, though this theory of meteors and comets is lucid and acceptable, the puzzle of Biela's Comet is not quite so easily explained. The German astronomer Wilhelm Klinkerfues of Göttingen, after viewing the meteor shower in

Galaxy in Andromeda.

1872, calculated the point at which the Bielids had appeared, and tracking them across the skies, concluded that Biela was not lost, but could be visible in the southern hemisphere. Accordingly, on November 30, 1872, he sent a telegram to the English astronomer N. Pogson, who was Government astronomer in Madras, India. The telegram, which reached India via Russia in a time variably reported as ninety-five minutes to an hour and thirty-five minutes (either time being quicker than it could possibly arrive today), read:

Biela touched Earth on 27th: Search near Theta Centauri.

Theta Centauri is a bright star in the southern hemisphere, which is not clearly visible in the United States and cannot be seen in Britain.

Pogson became excited himself and made a search. It was cloudy and rainy, but on the third morning he saw Biela through what he called "a brief blue space," and recorded it as "circular, bright, with a divided nucleus but no tail and about 45″ in diameter." This was, he said, in strong twilight. However on the next morning he was able to get a much clearer look: "This time my notes were: circular, diameter 75″, bright nucleus, a faint but distinct tail 8′ in length and spreading... I had no time to spare to look for the other comet, and the next morning clouds and rain had returned. For the next three mornings the sky was quite overcast and afterwards the comet would rise in daylight and could not therefore be observed."

Klinkerfues satisfied himself that it was indeed Biela that Pogson had seen. Or at least that it was one of Biela's two heads. Other astronomers thought that possibly Pogson had seen one Biela on one day, and the other Biela on the next day. And that the meteor-shower seen in Europe on November 27 was unquestionably due to the passage near Earth of a meteoric trail following in the track of the comet.

A writer in the *Edinburgh Review* in 1882, pointed out that when, in 1832, it had first been suggested that Biela could collide with Earth, Sir John Herschel had agreed that such a possibility existed, that it could be a dangerous collision, and that, taking into account the intersection of the orbits of the Earth and the Comet such a collision would in all likelihood take place within some millions of years.

Now, the writer went on, in 1882 it could be noted that the feared collision *had* actually taken place, on November 27, 1882, and that the result for Earth was nothing more than a magnificient display of fireworks! Nevertheless it was nothing less than amazing that Klinkerfues should have glimpsed the brush of the Comet's tail, so to speak, that he had so promptly and cleverly resorted to the use of the telegraph, communicating almost instantly with the other side of the world, and that he had been able to alert Pogson to see "the vagrant luminary" just as it was whisking off into space near the star Theta Centauri — this affair, taken all in all, was, in the words of the *Edinburgh Review*, "quite without a parallel in the experience of science."

Since 1882 there has been expressed a good deal of doubt that the comet which Pogson unquestionably saw was really Biela. Pogson was an experienced and dependable astronomer, so there is no question that he did glimpse at least one comet. But the tendency today is to believe that the meteor shower on 27 November 1872 was the last gasp of a dead Biela and that Klinkerfues and Pogson saw a coincidental comet.

But what of Biela II? Did that small comet too expire in a beautiful show of fireworks? Or is it possible that Biela's offspring, following its own, shorter path through space, an ellipse of lesser dimension than its parent's, intersected with Earth's orbit a year before Biela I? If that happened, the collision was the cause of more than a magnificent display of fireworks; indeed, it carried the danger that Sir John Herschel had said it would, and it came millions of years earlier than expected.

15

Central Siberia
June 30, 1908
7:17 A.M.

Thirty-seven years after the great fires in the Midwest, June 30, 1908 dawned a normal Tuesday in the densely forested basin of the Podkamenneya Tunguska River in Central Siberia, not far from the Arctic Circle. The region was sparsely populated by nomadic tribesmen called the Tungus or Evenki, who lived by raising reindeer and by hunting and trading furs.

At about 7:17 in the morning an unusual sight was seen streaking across the sky, from the southeast to the northwest. It was later variously described as "a red flying ball, with rainbow bands around it and behind it," a "radiance with green, red and orange streamers as broad as the street," an "irregularly-shaped brilliantly white, somewhat elongated mass," and "an elongated flaming object" with a broad front part and a narrower tail end. One witness spoke of "wedge-shaped rays" colored a bright fiery-red, flying toward the north with the broad end downwards.

Some people said it was brighter than the Sun, but most said they could look at it with the naked eye.

It was a hot, dry morning and as the body touched the horizon, it seemed to pulverize: there were several sharp reports like gun-shots, or the falling of stones, and a loud explosion. A huge cloud of black smoke arose, through which ran a forked tongue of fire. People said the sky was cut in two by flame. The explosion was deafening: the ground shook violently, the tents of the Evenki flew apart, and the people inside were propelled out onto the ground so roughly that several lost consciousness. Shortly afterward a great wave of heat washed over the area: one man said he thought his shirt was on fire; another felt a "fierce heat" scorch his ears. He said a hot wind had blown from the north at the moment that the sky had "opened"; it left little paths on the ground, and damaged the onion plants. There was a loud roaring sound, like thunder, in the north.

Seven hundred miles away, an engineer felt his locomotive jolt. He stopped the train for an inspection, but nothing could be found to explain the jolt.

The Evenki, shocked by the explosion and the sudden wave of heat, were then hit by a wind of hurricane intensity that smashed windows in villages as far as fifty miles from the site of the explosion. People ran in panic into the unpaved streets, while old women lifted their voices in lamentation. Surely, they said, it was the end of

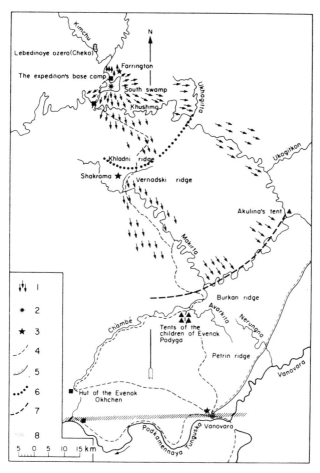

The Tunguska region affected by the collision, including:
1) forest destroyed; 2) point of impact; 5) road to the
Strelka trading station; 6) extent of scorched earth;
7) extent of forest destruction; 8) extent of explosive effect.

the world! In the gold mines the constructions creaked and groaned, the ground trembled, there was a loud roar and fainter crashes. The gold-washing equipment shook, dust rose from the ground, horses fell to their knees, and china slid off the shelves. The miners rushed out in terror.

One man who was ploughing his land on a hillside heard bangs like gun-fire; he saw a flame shooting up in the north sky above the forest. His horse fell to its knees, the fir forest was bent by a gigantic wind, and he had to hold his plough with both hands to keep it from blowing away. It was later estimated that, in order for him to have seen it from his hillside, the tongue of flame would have to have been about seven miles high.

Fortunately no people were killed, but roughly a thousand reindeer and many dogs were destroyed or frightened away, and stores of flour were burnt. It was later discovered that seven hundred and twenty square miles of forest had been destroyed in the river basin area: trees were burnt, scorched and torn out of the ground by their roots. They lay in a radial position, with their tops facing away from what must have been an incredibly massive concussion, an event of unparalleled violence.

Hundreds of miles away a university seismograph registered an earthquake. Instruments at meteorological stations recorded the intense air waves of a cataclysmic explosion. The sound waves traveled twice completely around the earth. But nobody knew what had happened.

In a vast area to the west of the devastated

forest, across Europe for a thousand miles or more, the sun set, but the night that ensued was a bright night, a night without darkness. On June 29th the sun had set at 9:15. But on June 30th, at ten o'clock, the sky was still bright. It was an irridescent night, rivalling the brilliance of the Northern Lights, not unfamiliar to people living in Arctic regions, but amazing to most Europeans. The sky shimmered brilliant red and yellow behind great glowing silver clouds. It was compared to the appearance of the sky following the explosions of the Krakatoa volcano in 1883.

In London the sky was tinted red to the northeast, and at midnight it was possible to read the small print of a newspaper in the glow. In Scotland, in rooms with windows that faced north, objects were seen to cast shadows. In Berlin the twilight was a greenish pale blue with a lacing of yellowish red, which dissolved around midnight to a red rim along the horizon. The sky was ruddy, as though it were reflecting a great fire, in Holland, Belgium, France, Sweden and throughout what was then the Austro-Hungarian Empire. In Russia a student took a photograph with his camera at midnight in the street of his town; the picture was published as an example of the incredible brightness of the atmosphere in the dead of night.

One Russian witness later recalled that at about 10 P.M. on that night of June 30th, he and his sister stood outside and saw a shining patch in the northeast part of the sky: its broad base rested on the horizon, and the upper part

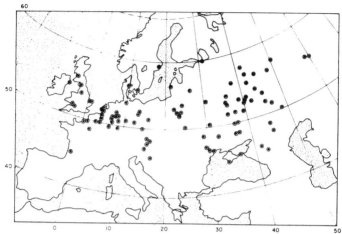

Map of the extent of the atmospheric phenomena after the Tunguska event. (From Zotkin).

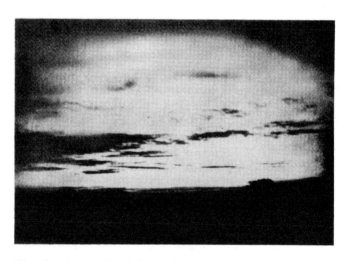

The glowing and shining skies above the Orlov province on the night of June 30th through July 1st, 1908.

tapered away quite high above it. The patch was milky white and gave off a steady light. A newspaper report said that on the night of June 30th, along the whole Baltic coast a "light silvery band shaped like an irregular arch covered as much as an eighth of the horizon and extended as much as ten degrees to the north."

In some places the glow grew brighter after midnight. When Wednesday, July 1st, dawned, the glow was gone. But it was back Wednesday night, although somewhat dimmer. After that, the sky returned to normal. But within two weeks the dust raised by the explosion was drifting over all of North America.

The sunsets in Chicago were beautiful that July: colors lingered on the horizon like luminescent curtains. No one apparently stopped to think that if the event responsible for this twilight beauty had occurred in or near Chicago instead of in the wilds of Siberia, the summer of 1908 would have seen another cataclysmic levelling of the City. If, in fact, the event had occurred in any city, or any area with a considerable population, the result would have been at least as bad as the great Chicago Fire of 1871.

In 1908 little information could be gotten out of Russia because of the unsettled political situation there, and because of the remoteness of the Tunguska region. It was known that a "fireball" had been seen in the sky and that there had been a violent shock, that reindeer herds had been decimated and trees uprooted. That was all. It was widely asssumed that a meteorite had crashed in the area; that was something that had been known to have happened. The first World War occupied everyone's attention until 1917, when the Russian Revolution provided further distraction. It was not until 1921 that L.A. Kulik, a geologist at the Mineralogical Museum of the Russian Academy of Sciences, who had been anxious to investigate the Tunguska "meteorite" for a long time, was able to go to Siberia himself and talk to witnesses.

He returned to Leningrad with a report and received funding from the Soviet Academy of Sciences to make an expedition into the region in 1927. When, after considerable difficulty, he reached what seemed to be the site of the explosion, he noted holes in the earth which he was confident would yield meteoritic matter. He made two more expeditions to the Tunguska in 1928 and 1929, but neither he nor any of the scientists with him could find any evidence of a meteorite. There was no crater and no debris. By late 1928 many eminent specialists had begun seriously to question Kulik's meteor theory: they pointed out that holes similar to those he was examining were often seen in peat bogs in various parts of Siberia.

After a third expedition, which left Leningrad on February 27, 1929, and which lasted for eighteen exhausting months, scientists interested in the Tunguska catastrophe became convinced that whatever had fallen on the Siberian wilderness, it had not been a meteorite. Kulik himself decided that he must have been working

Leonid Kulik

in the wrong area. He also began to talk about an explosion, which he had not previously considered, and for the first time he mentioned the possibility that the "meteorite" might somehow have been involved with a comet. On July first, 1908, he said, the Earth was passing the plane of the orbit of the Pons-Winnecke Comet. He thought that the white nights of June 30th and July 1st might have been caused by dust from a comet.

Others were now thinking along these lines. In 1934 the noted American astronomer F.L. Whipple gave a talk before the Royal Meteorological Society in London in which he said that since the white nights had been limited to Northern Europe, he believed that the cosmic object had a tail which had been suspended by the atmosphere of Earth and which had reflected sunlight all night.

Discussions and expeditions continued throughout the nineteen-thirties, until they were interrupted by the Second World War. Kulik himself was wounded, taken prisoner, and died on April 14, 1942. After the War investigations were resumed. Soil specimens brought back by Kulik were examined with new instruments, and the presence was discovered of nickeliferous iron and silicate components: it was known that the nucleus of a comet contains these components as well as ice and gases. A new expedition in the summer of 1958 offered conclusive evidence that the cosmic object had exploded in the air, high above the ground.

This explosion in the atmosphere, along with the two bright nights after the fall, the high speed at which the cosmic body was seen moving across the sky, the descriptions of the object itself, and the absence of any crater or sign of a meteorite has convinced reputable astronomers that a small comet had crashed into the Earth in 1908. It is the only possible deduction from available evidence. And it is the only recorded fall of a comet to Earth.

It is possible that this collision was connected with the Pons-Winnecke Comet which has a period of eighteen years, and which Kulik had noted was expected in the vicinity of Earth in 1908. It could not be known what effect the planet Jupiter had had upon this Comet during its last passage. If Jupiter had caused the Comet's path to be deflected significantly, then on the morning of June 30, 1908, the Comet could have been closer to Earth than ever before. We must remember, in addition, that any cosmic accident can, as we have seen, cause a fragment to break off from a comet and to develop its own cometary path.

In any case, whichever comet it was, if it crossed Earth's orbit at the exact instant that Earth was moving through that point itself, as seems to have been the case, the paths of the comet and of Earth would be a right angles to each other. The comet, traveling at a speed of twenty-five miles per second, with a mass of a million or more tons, would plunge into the atmosphere of Earth at a low angle, about seven degrees above the horizontal, coming from the southeast. At that angle it would have to pass through far more of the Earth's atmosphere than if it had come in at a more vertical angle.

The comet's head would become incandescent because of friction with the atmosphere and create a streak of light which moved, to the astonishment of all who saw it, across the morning sky. The coma, the misty shroud which encases the comet's nucleus, would vaporize in the course of the journey, so that by the time the comet was twenty miles or so above the ground, only the nucleus would remain: twenty thousand tons of its original million tons of weight, all of it intensely hot. The internal gases of the nucleus would expand rapidly.

Therefore at a point about twenty miles above the great forest in Central Siberia the nucleus would explode. There would be a great flash of flame in the sky, and a wave of radiant energy — the same infra-red radiation that carries heat from the Sun through the vacuum of space — would travel at one hundred and eighty-six thousand miles a second, the speed of all electro-magnetic energy, and strike the Earth in a fraction of a second, decimating the forest, scorching bodies and setting fire to supplies. This heat would be most intense in areas just below the point of explosion, but it would diffuse rapidly so that little heat would be felt more than a few miles away.

Then as the expansion of the gases in the comet's nucleus caused a sudden, powerful pressure on the gases in the molecules that make up Earth's atmosphere, there would be a great compression wave in the air, in which molecules of air and of hot explosive cometary gases would rush outward at more than seven hundred miles an hour. The striking of this wave against the Earth would generate sound waves that could be heard as far away as five hundred miles, and the impact — felt by a train seven hundred miles away — would register as an earthquake. The great winds this wave would generate would be of hurricane velocity.

When the initial blast struck the Earth twenty miles directly below the exploding nucleus of the comet, the powerful compression wave knocked down a great forest of ancient trees, completely devastating a circular area thirty miles in diameter at it widest point. Over an area of about seven hundred square miles, all the trees were torn out by their roots and lay pointed away from the center of the blast. The earth's surface was scorched by hot gases.

This comet came from the south and at 7:17 A.M. the Sun was in the east. Since the tail of a comet always points away from the Sun, this comet's tail had to have been extended toward the west. It would then be at right angles to the path of the comet's head as it entered the Earth's atmosphere. The tail would stretch westward from Siberia more than a thousand miles across Europe, producing the brightness that amazed everyone on those June nights in 1908.

The tail would drift high above Earth, unable to penetrate the atmosphere. The great mass of

Almost 20 years after the blast, Kulik found a cluster of trees still standing at what was evidently the center of destruction. Intensely hot air had scorched the forest for miles, but the comet had not exploded on the ground.

the comet's head would have burned its way downward, but the tail would float tenuously on the edge of the atmosphere, its substance creating a luminous ceiling over northern Europe. All night it would reflect the Sun's light.

We have gone into considerable detail about the cataclysm on the Tunguska river basin, because it provides proof that at least once, in our own century, a comet about which little or nothing is known collided unexpectedly with Earth. So unexpected was this collision that for years it was misinterpreted as the crash of a meteorite. The effects were catastrophic but contained, because of the nature of the territory over which the comet fell. And because the territory was relatively static, and because scientific techniques in this century have advanced rapidly, it was possible to search the area for evidences of the catastrophe.

This was not, of course, possible in Chicago, Michigan or Wisconsin in the late nineteenth century. If there is some fragment buried deep in the earth of Wisconsin or Michigan which could betray a cosmic visitor, no one has looked for it.

Many astronomers think that Biela's Comet is dead. It is conceivable, of course, that its head, unseen for a hundred years, still plies its course through the Solar System. Its coma and the gases that provided its spectacular tail are no doubt dissipated in any case. In 1843 when it was still a great Comet, flashing in its full glory across the sky, it moved one M. Lattey to publish a poem to it, in *The Illustrated London News*:

> Lone Wanderer of the trackless sky!
> Companionless! Say does thou fly
> Along thy solitary path
> a flaming messenger of wrath —
> Warning with thy portentous train
> Of earthquake, plague and battle-plain?

The answer to this question M. Lattey found evident. It was No:

> Some say that thou dost never fail
> To bring some mischief in thy tail
> For ignorance doth ever see
> Wrapped in its vain credulity
> Coupled some dire mishap with thee.

But it was perhaps ignorance which did *not* see the possibility of a dire mishap in the solitary path of these Lone Wanderers. Certainly a flaming messenger of wrath brought earthquake at least to Siberia on June 30, 1908, and death came wrapped in flames across the American Midwest one dry Sunday evening in October of 1871.

Bibliography

Angle, Paul. *The Great Chicago Fire*. Chicago: Chicago Historical Society, 1971.

Ball, Sir Robert. *The Story of the Heavens*. New York: Funk & Wagnalls, 1886.

Brandt, John C. and Maran, Stephen P. *New Horizons in Astronomy*. New York: W.H. Freeman & Co., 1979.

Chambers, George F. *The Story of the Comets*. Oxford, England: The Clarendon Press, 1909.

The Chicago Times, October 18, 1871 and October 19, 1871.

The Chicago Tribune, October 5, 1871 and October 18, 1871.

Donnelly, Ignatius. *Ragnarok: The Age of Fire and Gravel*. New York: University Books, 1970 (reprint of 1883 edition).

Goodspeed, Edgar Johnson. *History of the Great Fires in Chicago and the West*. Chicago: J.W. Goodspeed, 1871.

Hoyle, Fred and Wickramasinghe, Chandra. *Diseases from Space*. New York: Harper & Row, 1980.

Krinov, E.L. *Giant Meteorites*. Elmsford, N.Y.: Pergamon Press, 1966.

Luzerne, Frank. *The Lost City (Through the Flames and Beyond)*. New York: Wells & Co., 1872.

Moore, Patrick. *Comets*. New York: Scribner's & Sons, 1973.

Nininger, Harvey Harlow. *Out of the Sky*. New York: Dover Publications, 1952.

Reminiscences of Chicago During the Great Fire. Chicago: The Lakeside Press, 1915.

Watson, Fletcher Guard. *Between the Planets.* New York: Doubleday & Co., 1962.

Wells, Robert W. *Fire at Peshtigo.* Camden, N.J.: Prentice-Hall, 1968. (Reissued 1973 by Wisconsin Tales and Trails, Inc., Madison, WI.)

Young, Charles A. *A Manual of Astronomy.* Boston: Ginn & Co., 1902.